A Catholic's Guide to
ROME

DISCOVERING THE SOUL
OF THE ETERNAL CITY

Frank J. Korn

Paulist Press
New York/Mahwah, N.J.

Photographs are from the private collections of the author and Rev. Eugene Kotter.

Cover and book design by Saija Autrand, Faces Type & Design

Maps by Frank Sabatté, C.S.P.

Copyright © 2000 by Frank J. Korn

Library of Congress Cataloging-in-Publication Data

Korn, Frank J.
   A Catholic's guide to Rome : discovering the soul of the eternal city / Frank J. Korn.
     p. cm.
   Includes bibliographical references.
   ISBN 0-8091-3926-X (alk. paper)
   1. Christian pilgrims and pilgrimages—Italy—Rome—Guidebooks.
2. Christian shrines—Italy—Rome—Guidebooks. 3. Rome (Italy)—Guidebooks. I. Title.
BX2320.5.I8 K67 1999
263′.04245632 21—dc21

                                           99-041189

Published by Paulist Press
997 Macarthur Boulevard
Mahwah, New Jersey 07430

www.paulistpress.com

Printed and bound in the
United States of America

Contents

For
Julia
Jacqueline
Steven
Gregory
John
(and any other grandchildren to come);
and for their mothers
(my dear daughters-in-law)
Jean
Denise
Anne

Acknowledgments

I wish to thank, with all my heart, His Eminence, John Cardinal O'Connor, for taking time from his demanding schedule to write a foreword for this book. I am grateful to my wife Camille for her meticulous proofreading and patient typing of the manuscript. Without her faithful assistance *A Catholic's Guide to Rome* would not have been possible. My indebtedness extends also to Donna Crilly of Paulist Press, for her fine editorial work and excellent suggestions. I wish to thank Father Lawrence Boadt for his confidence in my knowledge of Rome, and my sons Frank, Ronald and John for their wise counsel. Lastly, I wish to extend my gratitude to a very special person, Emma Gatto. *(Requiescat in pace.)* Across the years, her wonderfully contagious enthusiasm for my every writing project kept me motivated.

Foreword

One of the great joys of serving the church as a cardinal is the possession of a titular church. Upon his reception of the "red hat," each cardinal is given a titular church in Rome by the Holy Father, a church that symbolizes the unbreakable bond and fervent devotion of each cardinal to the Holy See. My own titular church, Ss. Giovanni and Paolo (Saints John and Paul), is one of unspeakable beauty and bounteous history. It was the titular church of my beloved predecessors, Terence Cardinal Cooke and Francis Cardinal Spellman. Before Cardinal Spellman, it was the titular church of Eugenio Cardinal Pacelli, who was elected Pope Pius XII in 1939. A treasure in itself, it is but one of the many treasures in Rome.

In his *A Catholic's Guide to Rome*, Professor Frank J. Korn provides an invaluable guide to the treasures of Christian Rome. Here the reader finds an explanation and history of all the churches, shrines, catacombs and important sites in the Eternal City. Rome is a fascinating city, rich in Christian art, architecture and culture. Indeed, Rome is "an embarrassment of riches." One might easily be overwhelmed by all that Rome has to offer to the pilgrim: so many churches, so many shrines, so much history, so many legends, so much faith!

In my fifty-plus years of priesthood and twenty years as bishop, archbishop and cardinal, I cannot count how many times I have been privileged to traverse the cobblestones and the piazzas of Rome, to visit the Blessed Sacrament in so many of the churches, to climb down into the many catacombs and to visit the Vicar of Christ, the Successor to St. Peter, the Bishop of Rome. Each trip to the Eternal City is yet another opportunity to see one more of its holy sites, to learn more of its pious history and to appreciate the fruits of two thousand years of God's grace operative in the geographical center of his church.

Indeed, it is the plurality of Rome's riches that makes Professor Korn's book so valuable. The pilgrim to Rome is immediately dumbfounded by all that lies before him. What is Rome's history? What is the history of Christianity in Rome? What places should I visit, and what must I know of the significance of each? Where was the blood of the martyrs spilled? All of those questions—and many more—are answered in *A Catholic's Guide to Rome*. In his well-organized and cogently written book, Professor Korn leads the reader on a pilgrimage through Rome. He unlocks the history, the details and the legends that make each aspect of the Eternal City accessible to the reader. Whether one has visited Rome already, is planning a trip or just wishes to know more of its abundance, *A Catholic's Guide to Rome* is a "must read."

Our Holy Father, Pope John Paul II, has declared the year 2000 a Holy Year. The Holy Father has invited all people to visit his See as the new millennium breaks upon us. Go to Rome, bring this book and discover the treasure that is Rome!

+John Cardinal O'Connor
Archbishop of New York
May 1999

Prologue

Christian Rome and the Holy Year

From as far back as apostolic times, Christians around the globe have yearned to make a pilgrimage to Rome, there to worship in the very See of St. Peter, to pray at the tombs of the martyrs, to descend into the catacombs in search of their spiritual roots. Even Saint Paul wrote, "I must go on and see Rome." Just why Rome was selected by God to be the seat of the Supreme Pontiff is a mystery beyond human comprehension.

Today as the church prepares to stride into the Third Millennium, it remains still possible for Christians everywhere to come to Rome and worship on the same property, to celebrate the sacred mysteries in—at least parts of—the same places where Peter and Paul did so. In their day there was no splendid ecclesiastical architecture. The faithful met in the homes of fellow believers, which indicates that there were at least some better-off Christians whose residences were large enough for meetings. In the East, Christians used the room high up under the roof which was most quiet and tucked away. In Rome and throughout the West, the assembly place was probably the dining room. The bathroom (or *piscina*) was used for baptisms. The word "baptistry" denoted a pool, and "baptism" immersion. We know these things from archeological evidence and from ancient documents, including the writings of St. Paul himself. In his letter to the Romans, the apostle states: ". . . Greet Prisca and Aquila . . . and the church that meets in their house" (16:3–5).

When the persecutions of the Christians were launched by the tyrannical and paranoid Nero, it soon became unsafe for the flock to continue these house assemblies. Often the priests chose to hold their liturgies secretly, in the subterranean cemeteries beyond the walls of the city.

The skyline of Rome, a profusion of church domes

After Constantine put a stop to the slaughter and the oppression with the Edict of Milan, Christians began to raise grand temples to their divine Master, often over what remained of the old house churches, as well as upon the tombs of the martyrs and above the presumed graves of St. Peter and St. Paul. Before the fourth century was out, imposing Christian churches had sprung up from the soil of Rome like flowers in the most fertile of gardens.

The Jubilee Year

In the centuries that followed, the prolific building of church structures changed forever the face and skyline of the Eternal City. Since the style of architecture changed every few centuries, the churches of Rome today offer examples of everything from Romanesque to Gothic to Renaissance to Baroque.

Seeking to inspire his scattered flock to come to the banks of the Tiber and make their profession of faith at the tombs of the apostles, Pope Boniface VIII declared A.D. 1300 as a Holy Year.

Like its Judaic precursor, the *Annus Jubileus*, Roman Catholicism's Holy Year was originally planned to be observed every one hundred years. In the Old Testament tradition it was designated as a time of special public life, with abstention from normal business affairs, the redistribution of property, the cancellation of debts and the liberation of slaves (see Lv 25:8).

Pope Boniface VIII adopted and adapted the Hebrew jubilee for use by the church as a time for pilgrimage and an opportunity to grow in personal sanctity. He declared that all Christians who made the journey to Rome in the year 1300 to pray at the tombs of the apostles, martyrs and saints would be granted a plenary indulgence. The poet Dante took part in the events in Rome that year and even describes in the *Divine Comedy* (Inferno, Canto XVIII) how throngs of the faithful descended on the Eternal City, heeding the call of the Holy Father, and how multitudes of the devout jammed the inns and crowded the streets.

The inaugural Holy Year met with such an enthusiastic response that future Jubilees were declared every fifty years, then every thirty-three years and, eventually, every quarter century. Pope Clement VI decreed that the second Jubilee Year be moved up from 1400 to 1350.

In one of his letters from the collection *Epistulae de Rebus Familiaris*, Petrarch discusses his pilgrimage to Rome for the *Annus Sanctus* of 1350: "How inspiring for a Christian to journey to that city which is like a heaven on earth, sanctified by the remains of martyrs beyond number, drenched in the precious blood of those early witnesses to the Truth." He speaks with deep emotion of the privilege "to roam at will from tomb to tomb rich with the memories of the saints, to visit at random the basilicas of the Apostles, with no other companionship than pious thoughts."

One anonymous written account of the 1450 observance describes the excitement and zeal of the pilgrims in this way:

How wonderful to witness the great throngs who came. The roads leading to Rome were so jammed with people they seemed like ants . . . When the Pope imparted his benediction, the square and the basilica were both filled to overflowing. The bridges over the Tiber groaned under the weight of the multitudes on their way, all day and all night long, either to or from St. Peter's.

This outpouring of fervor prompted Pope Paul II to announce in 1470 that henceforth a Holy Year would be observed every twenty-five years, commencing with one in 1475. In the Jubilee of 1500, the opening of a Holy Door in St. Peter's and in the other three patriarchal basilicas (St. Mary Major, St. John Lateran, and St. Paul's Outside the Walls) was added to the rituals, not only to facilitate the flow of pilgrims and penitents but also to symbolize the special Holy Year indulgence.

The opening of the Holy Door in St. Peter's is dramatized with much pageantry. A Holy Year begins on the vigil of Christmas. The Holy Father, accompanied by a procession of cardinals and bishops, approaches the door and with a silver hammer taps on it, chanting *Aperite mihi portas justitae*, "Open the doors of justice for me." He strikes it again, chanting "I shall enter thy house, O Lord." A third time he knocks and sings "Open the doors because God is with us." At this point, inside the basilica, workmen lower the enormous block of concrete which has sealed the door for the past quarter century. The Vicar of Christ now kneels on the threshold and intones the solemn hymn *Te Deum Laudamus*, "We praise Thee, O God." He rises and enters the great church. The Holy Year is underway.

Millions of pilgrims are anticipated in Rome for the Holy Year. They will come upon the same sacred edifices that stirred the souls of our Christian forebears in that first Holy Year and have dazzled the eyes of pilgrims across the ages.

But "Christian Rome" is not confined merely to the churches. Evidence of the triumph of Christianity over the forces that sought to crush it is apparent everywhere in the Eternal City. Five centuries of the Roman Empire and the first five hundred years of the church run side by side. Thus in the old imperial capital one finds traces of Christianity literally "all over town." The imprint of the gospel or the stamp of the papacy can be found in every piazza, in every museum, on every fountain, on pagan ruins, on the Tiber's bridges, on Renaissance artworks, in the names of streets and restaurants and hotels, in the symbol of the cross that crowns every obelisk, in the archangel that stands atop the tomb of Hadrian and in the concerto of church bells that fills the air all day.

Christian pilgrims will discover traces of their rich spiritual heritage up on the Janiculum Hill, down in the Campus Martius, out on the Appian Way and aloft in the picturesque hill towns that surround Rome. Even the leading bank bears the name *Santo Spirito*, and one of the popular wines is called *Lacrima Christi* (tears of Christ).

The Pantheon is now a church, the gates are named for saints, the Colosseum hosts the Stations of the Cross on Good Friday evening. Where senators in purple-edged togas once strode, now walk cardinals in cassocks with red piping. Relics of most of the apostles are reputed to repose here in Rome. The catacombs, now silent and abandoned, were the first battleground of the Christian faith's struggle to survive here in the vaunted capital city. The days of the Caesars have vanished; the roars of the arena have subsided. The Roman eagle no longer soars. Pagan Rome is no more. The once hunted, hounded, despised, tortured and martyred Christians eventually and peacefully conquered Rome and continue to reign here in the person of the Vicar of Christ.

There is scarcely a brick in Rome that does not attest to that fact. It is my purpose to show the pilgrim how to find our Christian heritage in Rome, not only in the basilicas and churches, but virtually everywhere. It is also my hope that this book will enable the armchair traveler to make a vicarious pilgrimage to the See of Peter.

Roma Christiana! Christian Rome! What an awesome subject. My prayer is that I may somehow, in the pages that follow, render it at least a small measure of justice.

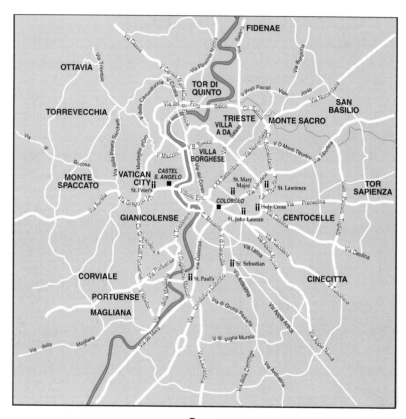

Rome

The Eternal City Of ?

*R*ome. The very sound of that word has thrilled, inspired, intimidated or antagonized humankind for twenty-eight centuries. Across that incredible span the ancient imperial capital has acquired numerous appellations such as Eternal City, City of the Seven Hills, City of the Caesars, City of the Popes, See of Peter, and so on.

There is a chance, however, that we do not know, and never will, the true name of this fabled place at all. A little-known tradition holds that Romulus and the other founding fathers took the secret of the city's original name with them to their graves. It seems that for identification purposes they agreed to let the city be called Rome after Romulus its first king, while not disclosing the actual name they had chosen. Only the Pontifex Maximus, Chief Priest, was permitted to pronounce the sacred name and this only before an altar while offering sacrifice, and in such a low whisper so as to render it inaudible to those in attendance. It was considered the gravest of sacrileges, punishable by death on a cross, for anyone to divulge the *nomen verum*. We learn these things from Pliny the Elder.

The motive for such mysterious goings-on was to block foes of the city from calling down upon it the curse and wrath of the gods. If such enemies did not know the real name of the city, the early Roman leaders reasoned, they could not very well invoke its ruin. In any event, until the secret of the name of that singularly beautiful city on the Tiber is unlocked, the venerable word "Rome" will simply have to do. Or should we revise that old familiar emblem, S. P. Q. R., to read: S. P. Q. _?

Ad Limina Apostolorum

I n addition to the names cited previously, another of Rome's numerous pseudonyms might be "Cemetery of the Apostles." The mortal remains of nine of them—eight of the original twelve plus Paul, who was conceded apostolic rank and prominence by the early church—are traditionally thought to have found their final resting place here.

As early as the late first century, pilgrims began to stream toward Rome to pray at the graves of the men who walked with Christ, those who set out soon after the events of that first Good Friday to preach the gospel and who became the first bishops of the church. It has long been a tradition of the church of Rome that Peter, "prince of the apostles," established the Christian community in the empire's capital, was martyred in Nero's circus in the Vatican meadows, and was interred in a potter's field just beyond the race course. Extensive and intensive archeological detective work beneath St. Peter's Basilica from 1939 until well into the 1960s led to the discovery of what are widely accepted to be the bones of the Fisherman of Galilee.

St. Peter's Basilica also houses the tomb where allegedly rest together the apostles Jude and Simon the Canaanite. They were thought to have preached together throughout Syria and Mesopotamia. After these travels, they went on to Persia where they shed their blood for the cause.

Paul, originally Saul of Tarsus, met his death in Rome by decapitation, out on the road to Ostia. The site of his burial was marked and preserved by the early believers. Over this site Constantine raised a great church, the venerable edifice known as St. Paul's Outside the Walls. To reach the tomb of the apostle Bartholomew, one must cross over the age-worn Pons Fabricius onto a small and congested little island in the Tiber. Here beneath the central altar of the church named for him, in a large sarcophagus flanked by ever-burning lamps, his body reposes. One of the most widely traveled of the twelve, Bartholomew took the gospel to such remote corners as India, Africa and Armenia. The modern name of the district where he died is Azerbaijan. His relics were transferred to Rome in the fourth century, most likely by order of the devout Empress Helena.

Matthias also toiled for a time in the spiritual vineyards of Armenia. Chosen as the replacement for the betrayer Judas Iscariot, he later went to Damascus. Some accounts have him dying at Phaleon in the province of Judea. Other sources suggest Jerusalem as the place of his martyrdom at the hands of an angry mob. Helena seems also to have directed that Matthias's remains be removed to Rome. Their final destination was to be the crypt below the papal altar of the Basilica of Santa Maria Maggiore. There is a dramatic effigy of Pope Pius IX kneeling before the tomb of St. Matthias.

Dismemberment of saints' bodies, so that relics might be distributed to a greater number of churches, was a common practice in the early centuries. Thus it is that some of Matthias's relics can also be found in the city of Trier in Germany.

The church of the Santi Apostoli, not far from Piazza Venezia, is said to contain the bodies of Philip and James the Less, placed there in a marble sarcophagus by Pope Julius I (337–352). The apse features a painting by Muratori of their martyrdom.

A highly-regarded account of the apostle Andrew, written in Greek, has him journeying to the foothills of the Caucasus Mountains to spread the Good News, thence to Byzantium, and finally on to Greece, a country with which his memory is still closely associated. At Patros his sermons incurred the wrath of the provincial governor who ordered the apostle crucified. When Constantius, son of Constantine, became emperor, he exhumed the body of Andrew and had it moved to the Church of the Holy Apostles in Byzantium. In 1460, during a Turkish invasion, the relics were taken to Italy for safekeeping. While the head of St. Andrew was returned by Pope Paul VI in 1964 to the See of Patros, a substantial portion of the remains are still venerated high atop the breezy Quirinal Hill in Bernini's architectural masterpiece, the Church of St. Andrew.

There is a church regulation that requires every diocesan bishop throughout the world to come to Rome at least once every five years to give a report on the state of his local church. Such visits are called *Ad limina Apostolorum*, "to the threshold of the Apostles." In light of all the possible apostolic entombments here, the phrase may be much more than a mere metaphor.

Domus Ecclesiae:
House-Churches

I n the first three hundred years of Christianity in the city of Rome, the more affluent among the faithful were the only ones who could provide the means, economic and otherwise, for organizing the Christian community. Some of them would put their homes at the disposal of their fellow believers for the celebration of eucharistic and baptismal rites, for use as centers of religious instruction and for the distribution of food and clothing to the needy.

In his letter to the Romans, St. Paul mentions one of these places of Christian worship—the congregation that meets in Prisca and Aquila's house. From this primitive type of *domus ecclesiae*, or house-church, there developed the *tituli*, or "titular churches," which served as a basis in the division into different groups of both clergy and laity that met on a regular basis, much like modern parishes today. Each meeting place took its name, or title (*titulus*), from the property owner. For instance, the house-church mentioned by Paul was known as the *Titulus Priscae*. A long-held tradition states that when Cecilia, a devout young woman, made her house available for purposes of worship, the bishop (Pope Urban I) officially dedicated it as the *Titulus Ceciliae*. By the end of the third century there were twenty-five such sites in Rome. In the centuries to follow, the Roman flock continued to honor the memory of these early benefactors. When in 313 the persecutions ceased, these houses were expanded into or replaced by splendid church edifices, but in nearly all of them the original name was retained. In fact, many of the former property owners were even held by the populace to be saints. Because the College of Cardinals had its origin in the clergy of the city of Rome in the early times of Christianity, each cardinal is still given "title" to a church in the Eternal City. A cardinal from a prosperous nation is expected to raise funds back home for the upkeep of his church in Rome.

During his episcopate in the Archdiocese of New York, Cardinal Francis Spellman was able to see to the direly-needed restoration of his ancient titular church, Santi Giovanni e Paolo on the Coelian Hill. In more recent years, Cardinal Bernard Law of Boston has done the same for his "Roman parish," Santa Susanna.

Let us now pay a brief visit to some of those historic churches in Rome, the See of St. Peter, that have their roots in the modest *domus ecclesiae* of apostolic times.

SANT ANASTASIA

This venerable basilica, formerly called the *Titulus Anastasiae*, is found at the foot of the Palatine Hill. Though its baroque facade dates to the seventeenth century, its history spans almost two thousand years. Beneath the high altar is an effigy of the virgin martyr Anastasia. St. Jerome is said to have offered mass here. Pope St. Gregory the Great made it a practice to distribute ashes here on Ash Wednesday. Excavation work below the church has revealed parts of the thick walls of the Circus Maximus.

SANTA MARIA IN TRASTEVERE *(Titulus Callisti)*

Tradition says that this church, which dates to pre-Constantinian times, was founded on a spot where a fountain of oil sprang out of the ground and ran down to the Tiber on the day our Savior was born. It is quite possible that the Christian liturgy was first publicly celebrated in Rome here, in the home of Callistus. Perhaps the earliest center of Marian devotion, this ancient place of Christian assembly may have been the first to be organized as a "parish church."

SAN CRISOGONO *(Titulus Chrysogoni)*

Documents from the fifth century show the signatures of several priests who presided over sacred rites at the "house church of

Chrysogonus." Over the modest residence, a sizable church was built by Pope Sylvester I (324–335). In 1123, through the efforts of its titular cardinal, Giovanni da Crème, the church was enlarged and given its handsome romanesque portico and lofty belltower. Twenty-two columns of Egyptian granite separate the graceful nave from the two side aisles. The apse is adorned with paintings of events in the life of Saint Chrysogonos, who converted hundreds of his fellow Romans to the faith.

SANTA CECILIA *(Titulus Ceciliae)*

This church and its patron saint are the subject of many popular legends. They maintain that in third-century Rome, in the Transtiberim precinct (now called *Trastevere*), there lived a young devout Christian girl by the name of Cecilia. Though born to all the luxury of the nobility, she had pledged her life to caring for the multitudes of sick and poor in the teeming neighborhood across the river from the main part of the city. She also spent a great deal of time at the sad task of burying her religious brothers and sisters who were being martyred almost daily.

The sixteen-year-old had vowed to remain forever a virgin as a sign of total dedication. As her confessor, Cecilia had the very Bishop of Rome himself, Pope Urban I, who encouraged her in her vocation. These plans were threatened, however, when her father arranged for his beautiful daughter to marry Valerian, a pagan nobleman. When the wedding day came, Cecilia sat apart from the guests, repeating psalms and prayers. After everyone had departed, the new bride implored the groom to honor the vow she had taken and to join her in working among the destitute and downtrodden.

At first angered, Valerian grew more and more impressed by Cecilia's obvious fervor and piety. A few days later he and his brother Tiburtius sought out the bishop, who was in hiding. From Urban the two men received instruction in the faith and then the sacrament of baptism. When word of their conversions reached the city's authorities, the brothers were arrested and subsequently executed for refusing to pay homage to pagan idols. The grief-stricken

Cecilia, after seeing to the entombment of Valerian and Tiburtius in the catacombs outside the walls, was herself soon ordered to appear before Almachius, the Prefect of Rome. She was arraigned on charges of practicing and promoting a forbidden cult. She was sentenced to death by suffocation, in the steam bath of her own home. But Cecilia survived a whole day of being locked in the tiny room filled with hot vapors. When the guards opened the door she stepped out unharmed, as though from a cool refreshing shower.

Almachius then sent a soldier to her home with orders to behead her. In vain the man attempted to carry out the task. Roman law stipulated that if a condemned person were to survive three blows of the executioner's axe, he or she was to be set free. No one ever did, until Cecilia. The terrified soldier fled, telling everyone he met about the "miracle." Local Christians rushed to the house and found Cecilia lying in a pool of blood, a deep gash on her neck, but still alive. For three days she lay there, preaching the gospel and singing sacred songs to hundreds of pagan visitors who had come to see for themselves. Great numbers of them converted on the spot.

On the third day Pope Urban arrived. After bequeathing the family mansion to him for use as a church, Cecilia passed away in utter serenity on November 22 in the year 230. In accordance with her wishes, her remains were placed in a crypt in the catacombs. The following day the pope declared her house a place of Christian assembly, designating it *Titulus Ceciliae*. To this day it has remained among the most prominent Christian sites in Rome.

In 821 Pope Paschal I set out to find the remains of the saint and transfer them to the church. But where they had been placed in the vast network of subterranean cemeteries was no longer known. One night, the pontiff had a dream in which he was told where to look. With some fellow clerics he went out the Appian Way to the Catacombs of Saint Callistus. They quickly came upon the crypt of Cecilia and opened it. Her body was still incorrupt six centuries after her death.

In 1599, as often happens in this city of legend, the story

of Saint Cecilia entered the realm of verified history. Cardinal Sfondrato, then in charge of the ancient basilica, ordered restoration work on the interior. He decided to move Cecilia's relics to a side chapel until completion of the work. He invited the sculptor Stefano Maderno to the opening of the tomb, instructing him to do a carving of what they would find. As had Pope Paschal, eight centuries earlier, Sfondrato and Maderno saw the intact body of the saint. Maderno produced the masterpiece still on view today at the main altar. The marble effigy shows the slender virgin lying on her side, her knees drawn together, her neck deeply gashed, her arms out in front of her, with her right hand extending three fingers, her left hand one. The inference is that in her last breath she continued to profess her belief in the Holy Trinity, that even in death she managed to bear witness to the faith.

Because she was known to have loved singing hymns—aloud or in her heart—Cecilia early on became known as the patron saint of music and musicians.

Today in this crowded, colorful, noisy district of medieval dwellings, produce markets, wine cellars, coffee bars, and narrow streets, where women still do the family wash in buckets at the public fountains and teenagers roar by on motor scooters, the Church of Saint Cecilia is an oasis of tranquility and beauty. One enters through a landscaped courtyard. In its center is a huge Roman *cantharus* of white marble, from which a thin jet of silvery water rises. The peach-colored front of the church rests on a portico of African marble columns. All this is a fitting tribute to the pretty girl who, like Mother Teresa in our time, brought such tenderness and love to "the poorest of the poor."

SANTI NEREO E ACHILLEO *(Titulus Fasciolae)*

This very old church, near the Baths of Caracalla, is mentioned in records as far back as the year 350. The name of the house owner is not known. *Fasciola* is Latin for bandage or wrapping. There is a legend that St. Peter, fleeing from the Mamertine jail, dropped here a bandage that had covered his wrist wounded by his chains. The pious Roman matron who lived here preserved the relic and then opened her dwelling to the local congregation.

SANTI GIOVANNI E PAOLO *(Titulus Bisantis)*

This church is named for a pair of wealthy brothers who had served as officials in Constantine's court. Converted to the new faith by the emperor's daughter Constantia, John and Paul hosted Christian rites in their handsome home on the Coelian Hill. When Flavius Claudius Julianus came to power in 360, he sought to restore the old pagan religion. Known to history as Julian the Apostate because he abjured Christianity, he ordered the brothers to reject Christianity and embrace the pagan deities. When John and Paul refused to comply, Julian had them executed in their own house on

Church of Sts. John and Paul (Santi Giovanni e Paolo) on the Coelian Hill

the night of January 26, 361. Friends claimed the victims' remains and interred them in the garden of the brothers' property. A short time afterwards, Julian had three more Christians decapitated for praying at the grave of John and Paul. These were Crispin, Crispianus and Benedicta. Thus it can be said that this *titulus* was truly bathed in the blood of martyrs.

In 398 a wealthy and influential senator, Pammachius, a close friend of St. Jerome, transformed the slain brothers' dwelling into a three-aisled church and named it the Basilica of Saints John and Paul. The fame of the two men was further perpetuated by the inclusion of their names among the very few listed in Eucharistic Prayer I.

In the late Middle Ages, under orders of Pope Adrian IV, the church was enlarged in the Romanesque style and given a new entrance portico of eight marble and granite columns. Adrian, the only Englishman to ascend the Chair of Peter, also erected an elegant campanile over the nearby remains of a temple to the ill-fated Emperor Claudius. Over the subsequent centuries, the church underwent many alterations and took on numerous additions.

In the 1700s the church was assigned to the care of the Passionist Fathers, founded by St. Paul of the Cross who lies entombed within the edifice. In 1887 Father Germano, a Passionist priest who had a deep interest and considerable expertise in archeology, began excavations with a meager budget and a handful of volunteers. Digging revealed the walls of a large apartment house built in the second century A.D. Further probing brought Father Germano into a series of painted rooms that give a vivid idea of how well-to-do Romans would have adorned their homes. The cellar, ground floor and second floor of the original dwelling were discovered in an excellent state of preservation. A small oratory with some of the earliest Christian paintings in Rome was also brought to light.

As one of Rome's early house-churches, *S.S. Giovanni e Paolo* is always entrusted to the stewardship of a member of the College of Cardinals. This was the titular church of Cardinal Eugenio Pacelli, who in 1939 became Pope Pius XII. Since then, the church has been under the care of the Archbishop of New York.

SANTI QUATTRO CORONATI *(Titulus Aemilianae)*

The acts of the synod of 499, called by Pope Symmachus, refer to this old place of Christian assembly near the Colosseum. The church subsequently erected here in the late fourth century was dedicated to four Roman soldiers: Severius, Severianus, Carpophorus, and Victorius. Having embraced the gospel, they denounced the worship of the pagan gods. They were scourged to death by order of Diocletian.

The church was reconstructed in the twelfth century by Pope Paschal II. The three-aisled interior is embellished by a coffered ceiling and thirteenth-century frescoes honoring the lives of the four martyrs.

SANTI MARCELLINO E PIETRO *(Titulus Marcellini et Petri)*

This ancient house of worship on the Via Merulana features an impressive cupola and baroque facade, thanks to Pope Benedict XIV (1740-1758) who, as Cardinal Prospero Lambertini from Bologna, was titular pastor here. The pious owners of the original house-church were martyrs under Diocletian in the late third century. Their bodies were buried on the Via Cornelia in the Vatican area.

SANTA PRASSEDE *(Titulus Praxedis)*

This pious girl, daughter of a prominent Roman senator, grew up along with her older sister Pudentiana in a household that hosted Peter, the first Bishop of Rome. The young women devoted their lives to the church, working among the poor and burying the remains of those slaughtered for their faith. Perhaps in later life, following her parents' example, Praxedes offered her house as a place of assembly for the faithful. Some priests from the *Titulus Praxedis* are mentioned in an epitaph dated 491 in a cemetery on the Via Tiburtina. Though tucked away in a narrow side street near the

Interior of Santa Prassede

Basilica of Santa Maria Maggiore, Santa Prassede's became a principal site of pilgrimage in the Middle Ages. The austere exterior stands in sharp contrast to the richly adorned interior. The nave and two side aisles are separated by sixteen granite columns taken from various pagan temples. The walls boast Renaissance paintings of the Passion of Christ. A large porphyry disc in the floor of the nave seals the well of the original house. Prassede is believed to have poured the blood of the martyrs into this well. In the *confessio*, the sunken area before the main altar, lie the mortal remains of the saintly sisters, which were transferred here by Pope Paschal I from the Catacombs of Priscilla.

Santa Prassede's is rich in mosaics, some of which decorate a closed-off chapel where the shaft of a marble column is preserved. This was brought to Rome from Jerusalem in 1223 with the claim that it was to this pillar that Christ was chained when he was scourged by the Roman soldiers.

SANTA PUDENZIANA *(Titulus Pudentia)*

On the southern slope of the Viminal Hill lived Quintus Cornelius Pudens, a prominent member of the Roman senate. A tradition that has come down from the earliest times of Christianity tells of a deep friendship that developed between the senator and St. Peter. The story relates that shortly after his arrival in the Eternal City—in A.D. 42—the Galilean fisherman not only began to conduct the sacred mysteries at the senator's palatial home, but also resided there for the next eight or nine years. Hence, the *Titulus Pudens,* as it eventually became known, can perhaps be said to have served as the first cathedral and the first papal residence.

A word that conjures images of Gothic splendor, statues, stained glass, and episcopal pomp and pageantry, *cathedral* derives from the Latin word *cathedra,* meaning chair. Thus, the cathedral of any diocese is that church which contains the bishop's official chair—that is, his throne. The ceremonial chair thought to have been used by Peter was eventually found in the house church of Senator Pudens. That humble wooden chair is now enshrined in the apse of the Basilica of St. Peter in the Vatican.

Senator Pudens—who is mentioned in St. Paul's Second Letter to Timothy—along with his wife Priscilla and their devout daughters, Praxedes and Pudentiana, were among the first converts of many thousands baptized by Peter in that very house. All of them became fervent in their wish to serve the church.

Priscilla came from the prominent patrician family of the Acilius Glabrio. She donated to the Christian community a huge portion of the land of her country villa, out on the Via Salaria, for use as a subterranean burial ground. The cemetery was named in her honor, *Catacumba Priscillae.*

One might say that the Titulus Pudens was also antiquity's "Vatican," because most major ecclesiastical and pontifical events of that era unfolded there. Every Eucharist celebrated by Peter was, in reality, a papal mass. Tradition holds that on this site the original Supreme Pontiff of the Church of Rome ordained to the priesthood the men who would be his three immediate successors: Linus,

Cletus and Clement. From here preachers of the gospel were sent forth by Peter to all corners of the known world. As the second century dawned, the Titulus Pudens became an increasingly popular site of pilgrimage. The intimate link of this church with the apostles endeared it to the faithful who wished to manifest their veneration and love for it.

In the year A.D. 145, Pope Pius built an oratory on the property and gave it the double name of *Ecclesia Pudenziana—Titulus Pudens*. Subsequent centuries witnessed dramatic expansion and beautification of this historic shrine, as well as a permanent name change—to Santa Pudenziana. Today, the church features a richly ornamented front, a handsome classic doorway and a ninth-century campanile—the loveliest bell tower in Rome. Perhaps the most beautiful facet of this architectural gem is the enormous mosaic covering the dome of the apse. Commissioned in 390 by Pope Siricus, the still-brilliant mosaic shows a senatorially-clad Christ flanked by the similarly garbed Peter and Paul. In the background stand two girls, Pudentiana and Praxedes, about to crown the apostles with wreaths of laurel. All of this may have been an effort at a powerful artistic expression of the new imperial dimension of the Christian Church. Just a decade earlier, in 380, the Emperor Theodosius had proclaimed Christianity as the official state religion.

As Christianity now stands poised on the threshold of its third millennium, it can boast of thousands of magnificent houses of worship in every country and on every continent of our planet. But if one wishes to pray in what might be the very first one of them all, one must come to Rome, to the southern flank of the Viminal Hill, to the house of Senator Pudens, the Church of Santa Pudentiana.

SANTA SUSANNA *(Titulus Gaii)*

According to an ancient tale, in the year 290, Susanna, the lovely eighteen-year-old daughter of the priest Gabinius and niece of saintly Pope Caius (283–296), was martyred in her home on this site upon the Quirinal Hill. Having refused to break her vow of virginity and marry Maximianus Galerius, heir and adopted son of

Santa Susanna

the Emperor Diocletian, Susanna was ordered beheaded. Her remains were buried in the catacombs of Saint Felicitas outside the city walls. Shortly thereafter, her uncle, the Pope, dedicated her home as a *titulus* church. There the early Christians would gather to celebrate the sacred mysteries—often at great risk when the persecutions were raging.

Sometime after the end of the anti-Christian violence, a church was built over Susanna's home and her remains were translated to the crypt beneath the main altar, where they still repose. Pope St. Gregory the Great (590-604) officially named it the Titular Church of *Sancta Susanna*. In 796 Pope Leo III renovated the building, adorning it with mosaics and adding a baptistry. Over the next few centuries, other restorations and embellishments were carried out. The structure we see today dates from the end of the sixteenth century. Its baroque front, the work of Carlo Maderno, is among the most beautiful and widely imitated in all of Rome. The interior has a sense of spaciousness, resembling a painted renaissance hall, full of light and awash with vivid colors. Six splendid frescoes, done by Baldassar Croce in 1600, allude to Susanna the virgin martyr and to the prophet Daniel's story of Susanna in the Old Testament. There are also frescoes of the evangelists and the doctors of the church. The church abounds in statuary, including carvings of Peter and Paul that flank the high altar, works of Vasoldo.

Ancient documents show that in 484 Cardinal Asello took charge of the church of Santa Susanna. As the centuries passed there were numerous distinguished successors to this post, some of whom eventually ascended the Chair of Peter. Pope Leo III (795-816), for example, was once the cardinal with the title to Santa Susanna's, as was Pope Nicholas V (1447-1455).

In 1921, Pope Benedict XV officially designated Santa Susanna as the American National Church in Rome and invited the Paulist Fathers, a community of priests founded in New York in 1858, to serve here, where they have been on duty ever since. In 1947 Cardinal Mooney of Detroit became the titular cardinal of Santa Susanna. Since then the historic church has been overseen by American prelates. From 1958 to 1970 Richard Cardinal Cushing of

Boston held the title. When Archbishop Humberto Medeiras of the same diocese was given the red hat in 1973, he was also given responsibility for this church. Today it remains under the jurisdiction of the Archbishop of Boston.

SAN CYRIACUS *(Titulus Cyriace)*

This church, along with its history, has faded into oblivion. All we know of it is its name.

SAN LORENZO IN LUCINA *(Titulus Lucinae)*

A pious Christian lady, Lucina, converted her house in the heart of old Rome into an oratory. We know of at least one papal election held here (A.D. 366—Pope Damasus). Documents from the conference of Symmachus in 499 mention the oratory.

Tradition maintains that Lucina hid Pope Marcellus in her home when he was being hunted down by the Emperor Maxentius during a persecution of the Christian community. Late in the fourth century a church dedicated to Saint Lawrence was erected over the ruins of the house of Lucina.

SAN MARCO *(Titulus Marci)*

This church is dedicated to Pope St. Marcellus, the same one sheltered by the matron Lucina from the Christian-hating Emperor Maxentius. On this site, along the present Via del Corso, the saintly bishop lived out his days, often hosting Christian assemblies. A letter from the city prefect written in the early part of the fourth century speaks of this place as the *ecclesia Marcelli*. A papal election was held here in 418, putting Boniface I in the Chair of St. Peter.

TITULUS DAMASI

No longer is anything known about the house-church of Damasus, beyond its name.

SAN MARTINO AI MONTI *(Titulus Equitii)*

Recent restoration work on this church has unearthed portions of the house-church that bore the *titulus* of Equitius in ancient times. Scholars now conclude that it was Pope Symmachus in the fifth century who had the deteriorating home of Equitius torn down and replaced with a fine romanesque church. A legend says that the Emperor Constantine was cured of a serious illness in this house-church by Pope Sylvester I.

Saint Martino's has been restored and altered many times during its long history. The facade one sees today dates to 1667, but the interior preserves the fifth-century aspect of Pope Symmachus's building.

SANT EUSEBIO *(Titulus Eusebi)*

The priest Eusebius daily hosted in his home (near today's Piazza Vittorio) the local Christian flock for mass and communion. Eusebius, not to be confused with the great church historian, was martyred under the Arian Emperor Constantius in 357. Shortly afterward Pope Liberius officially consecrated the house as the *Titulus Eusebi.* Pope Zacharias enlarged the church in the eighth century and Leo III did likewise in the ninth. The architect Stefano Fontana constructed the harmonious facade in 1711. On January 17 of each year the Romans bring their pet animals to be blessed on the steps of Saint Eusebius. Cabbies bring their horses and carriages.

SAN VITALE *(Titulus Vestinae)*

Sometime in the third century a small chapel was built on the slopes of the Viminal Hill to honor the martyred brothers Gervasius and Protasius. A rich woman, Vestina, gave huge sums of money to beautify the chapel and redesign it into a sizable basilica. Pope Innocent I (401–417) officially named the site Titulus Vestinae in recognition of the benefactress. It was during the pontificate of Gregory the Great (590–604) that the church was given the name Saint Vitalis, to honor the pious father of Gervasius and Protasius.

The exterior of the fifth-century church remains remarkably preserved. The portico of four columns and the apse both belong to the original structure. Pope Innocent would easily recognize it, but perhaps be confused by the fact that this once ground-level church now has to be approached by a descending flight of thirty-four steps, due to the stratification of the Eternal City across two millennia.

SAN PIETRO IN VINCOLI *(Titulus Aostoli)*

When the Empress Eudoxia, wife of Valentinian III, wished to erect a church to house the chains *(vincoli)* of St. Peter, she chose this site of early Christian worship. The impressive basilica we visit today is largely the work of Pope St. Sixtus III (432–440) and typical of the church architecture of the time, with three aisles separated by massive marble columns. In the *confessio*, before the high altar, is the reliquary, a glass casket containing the chains said to have been attached to the apostle's wrists and ankles during his imprisonment. This church is also renowned for housing one of the greatest works of art of all time, the colossal statue of Moses, by Michelangelo.

The Vatican: *Ecco Roma!*

Eight centuries before Christ, there reigned over the primitive village of Rome a soothsaying king named Numa Pompilius. Whenever this successor to Romulus, the founding monarch, wished to declare to the people his *Vaticinia*, supposed messages from the gods, he would cross the Tiber and climb the low hill that rose out of the meadows there, whence he spoke. From this ritual the area took its name *Ager Vaticanus*.

Yet with all his gifts of prophecy, the gentle sovereign could never have foreseen that, almost three thousand years later, these meadows would comprise the territory of the world's tiniest country, be the seat of the universal church and the residence of its Pontifex Maximus. Welcome to Vatican City!

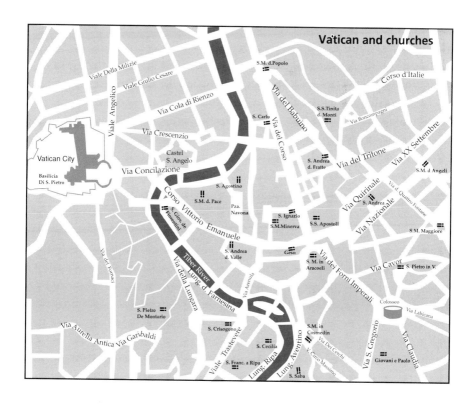

After ending the persecutions, Constantine granted the state-owned Lateran Palace to Pope Miltiades for use as his official episcopal residence. He also commissioned the construction of a cathedral (St. John's) adjacent to the palace. At the same time he ordered a splendid basilica (St. Peter's) to be built directly over the presumed site of the apostle's grave.

The centuries rolled by, the empire crumbled, and the people proclaimed their spiritual leader, the pope, their secular ruler as well. In 754 the church and the city were subjected to constant merciless sieges by the Lombard tribes, prompting Pope Stephen III to journey across the Alps to seek the aid of the powerful Frankish king, Pepin. The sympathetic Gaul, a Christian himself, at once sent armies to rout the Lombard intruders. With peace restored, Pepin then gave to the pope a vast expanse of land in northern Italy to buffer the Holy See of Peter against future invasions. Known as the Papal States, this territory extended across the regions of Latium, Umbria, the Marches, Emilia and Romagna, covering an area about twice the size of Massachusetts. The Lateran remained the seat of the papacy until the dawn of the 1300s when Pope Clement V and his successors, up to and including Gregory XI, chose to reign from Avignon, a town on the banks of the Rhone in southern France. In 1376, persuaded by the arguments of a Dominican tertiary, Catherine of Siena, that the only rightful place for the See (from Latin *sede*, or seat) of Peter was Rome, Gregory XI returned with his court to the Eternal City. He decided to reside not at the Lateran but instead in the Vatican, which had been fortified with soaring walls in the 800s by Leo IV. For this reason, Vatican City is still called by the people of Rome *La Citta Leonina*.

Throughout the ensuing eras—the late Middle Ages, the Renaissance, and the Baroque—the pope continued in his dual capacity as head of the church and king of the Papal States. In the nineteenth century, however, the fever of unification swept over Italy and with the Italian revolution, *Il Risorgimento*, the new powers confiscated the Papal States, leaving the pope with just the Vatican from which to conduct the business of the worldwide church.

This resulted in an estrangement between the papacy and the

Italian State until the Lateran Treaty was signed in 1929, resulting in Italy's recognition of Vatican City as an independent state, with the Holy Father as its sovereign. The pact also ceded extraterritorial autonomy to various church properties in and around Rome, such as the basilicas of St. John, St. Mary Major and St. Paul's Outside the Walls. The same extraterritorial status was granted to the subterranean early Christian burial grounds, the catacombs, and to the papal residence at Castel Gandolfo in the nearby Alban hills.

Today we find within the mighty walls of Rome a diminutive walled-in "country of the spirit," the Vatican. Despite its Lilliputian dimensions, 108 acres, *Il Vaticano* has all the trappings of statehood—an army (the Swiss Guard), a railroad, a postal system, a currency, a flag, a national anthem and, most importantly, diplomatic relations with more than a hundred nations, including the United States, and in the near future most likely Israel as well.

While it is intriguing to note the accoutrements of statehood the Vatican possesses, it is equally fascinating to consider the basics of everyday life *not* found there. Walk the streets and backalleys of the Vatican and you will not find a hotel, a hospital, a restaurant, a dry cleaners, a barbershop, a factory, a ballpark, a high school or a movie theater. In fact, there is just one bar, and strangely enough it is inside St. Peter's near the sacristy. This clerical gathering place offers coffee and tiny sandwiches to priests, hungry and thirsty after saying mass at one of the basilica's many altars.

During the fabled "Grand Tour" of the 1700s, weary travelers were reinvigorated when the coach and horses had labored up the last rise of the Via Flaminia and the coachman paused to point in the distance to the great dome of St. Peter's, rising high over the rooftops, and cried out *Ecco Roma!* Behold Rome!

Across the last quarter century, my wife and I have made more than fifty trips to Rome. Upon our every return there, after our drive in from Da Vinci Airport, when at last we catch sight of the dazzlingly white cupola floating in the Roman sky, we cannot help but echo the old coachman's cry: *Ecco Roma!*

Old St. Peter's

Christmas Day in Rome, in the year 800: the interior of St. Peter's Basilica is awash in the flickering light of myriad candles. An immense throng of cardinals, bishops and clergy, of kings, princes and barons, of diplomats, dignitaries and ordinary citizens fills the vast church and spills out into the forecourt.

The wooden rafters echo with the celestial singing of the *Schola Cantorum*, as his holiness Pope Leo III descends from the papal altar to place a crown sparkling with gems on the head of Charlemagne, kneeling at a *prie dieu* in the center aisle. The pontiff then puts upon the shoulders of this great benefactor of the Holy See a purple robe, declaring Charlemagne the first emperor of the Holy Roman Empire. The basilica now resounds with the happy chant of the entire congregation: "To Charles, the most pious Augustus, crowned by God! To our great and peace-loving Emperor, long life and victory!"

For those readers who have been to Rome and have stood in St. Peter's Basilica, yet cannot recall any wooden rafters, let me point out that this historic event took place not in the baroque creation of Bramante and Michelangelo, but rather in the "old St. Peter's." Many visitors to the Eternal City today fail to realize that the great church upon Vatican Hill is the second to have occupied that site.

In A.D. 90, twenty-three years after Peter the Apostle, the first Bishop of Rome, was interred in Vatican soil, Pope Cletus erected a small oratory over the grave. This chapel became at once the center of the primitive Christian church and the object of universal veneration among the early believers.

A little more than two centuries later, after he himself had embraced Christianity, Constantine commissioned the construction of a magnificent romanesque basilica directly over the oratory of Cletus. The *Liber Pontificalis Ecclesiae Romanae* reports: *Augustus Constantinus fecit basilicam Beato Petro Apostolo* (The august Constantine erected a basilica to the blessed Peter). It also tells how Constantine himself, having removed his crown and picked up a shovel, filled the first twelve receptacles with soil and carted them away on his shoulders in honor of the twelve apostles.

Begun in 324, consecrated in 326, but not completed until 349, old St. Peter's had five aisles, the nave separated from the four side aisles by columns supporting an architrave. The basilica measured almost three hundred feet in length and just over a hundred feet in width. Five doors, corresponding to the five aisles, led into the interior which featured, in addition to the main altar, more than a hundred smaller ones. The central door was dignified with this appellation above it: *Limen Apostoli* (The Threshold of the Apostle).

Our knowledge of the appearance of the first St. Peter's Basilica is based chiefly on the plan and description drafted by Tiberius Alferanus while it still stood, and on the notes and sketches left by several other writers. These ancient drawings show a church richly embellished by frescoes, mosaics, statues, and gold and silver lamps and candelabra. St. Peter's, with its mosaic facade, was approached by a flight of thirty-five steps leading to a terrace where the devout would often be seen advancing on their knees, holding lighted candles.

At the end of the terrace, three ornamental doors opened onto a colonnaded atrium called the *paradise*, planted with palms and olive trees about a center fountain in the shape of a colossal bronze pine cone. This fountain is now displayed in the Vatican's sprawling Courtyard of the Pine. The forecourt also featured twin fountains that cooled and freshened the air and slaked the thirst of multitudes of visitors. Here too were stalls where pilgrims could purchase food and devotional objects.

Such was the veneration and awe in which St. Peter's was held that during the various barbarian invasions in the twilight of Imperial Rome, this site remained inviolable. We know that Alaric with his Goths, Vitiges with his Longobards, and Genseric with his Vandals ransacked and looted all of the city's churches. But these same crude, savage intruders, though well aware of the artistic treasures of St. Peter's Basilica, could not bring themselves to desecrate it, nor molest the droves of people who had taken refuge there.

Even for old St. Peter's, however, days of storm eventually came. In 846, when the Saracens invaded Rome, the Constantinian basilica was plundered and seriously damaged, and for the first time even the tomb of St. Peter was profaned. When in the 1300s the See of Peter was transferred to Avignon in the south of France, the basilica fell into a state of almost total neglect and abandonment. Wooden ceiling beams sagged; the masonry began to crack. Doors torn from their hinges by violent weather were left unrepaired, vegetation sprouted from breaks in the flooring, and sheep and other animals roamed in and out at will.

When Gregory XI brought the papacy back to Rome in 1376, he sought to restore St. Peter's Basilica to its former splendor. The toll on the fabric of the church, however, proved fatal. The left wall had begun to buckle. In 1450, alarmed papal architects advised Pope Nicholas V that collapse now menaced the ancient sanctuary.

In 1492 Bernardo Rossellino tried valiantly to shore up the church but sadly concluded that it was by then in an irreversibly ruined condition. When Giuliano della Rovere ascended the Throne of Peter as Pope Julius II in October of 1503, one of his first acts was to order the first St. Peter's Basilica pulled down and construction on its replacement begun at once. Thus it was that twelve centuries of solemn service to the Christian world were swept away by the wrecker's ball. The first stone of the new church was set in place by Pope Julius in April of 1506.

Today every wide-eyed visitor to beautiful St. Peter's Basilica would do well to pause a moment to reflect on, and try to see in the mind's eye, the majestic romanesque edifice which once stood for so long on that very spot.

Basilica of St. Peter

The New St. Peter's Basilica

Upon arriving in Rome, all pilgrims have as their top priority and most fervent wish a visit to the greatest architectural symbol of Christianity—the venerable Basilica of Saint Peter that rises over what many believe to be the burial site of the prince of the Apostles. On the spot where Peter had been laid to rest in the year 67, St. Anacletus, his third successor as Bishop of Rome, built a small oratory, *Memoria Sancti Petr.* The humble shrine that marked his grave became the object of universal veneration. Christians—first from throughout the city, then from all over Italy and Europe—came here to honor the fisherman from Galilee, the man who walked with our Lord, the man commissioned by Christ to build his church on earth. They are still coming even as we approach the third millennium of that church.

It is altogether appropriate, then, that the Basilica of St. Peter be the greatest house of worship in all of Christendom, in splendor and tradition. For on this holy ground and with this magnificent temple, we are in truth exalting not Peter, but rather Christ himself through Peter.

Upon crossing the Tiber over the Victor Emmanuel Bridge, today's pilgrims find themselves suddenly on a Parisian-style boulevard, the *Via della Conciliazione*, built by Mussolini to commemorate the reconciliation reached between the church and the Italian State in the Lateran Treaty of 1929. Looming into view directly ahead is the fabled dome they have seen all their lives—in textbooks, in magazines, in slides, in movies, on postcards and on television: St. Peter's Basilica in the Vatican! At the top of the boulevard, the excited hordes of first-time visitors step into St. Peter's Square and are at once swept up in the wondrous colonnade designed by Bernini to suggest the arms of Mother Church. The poet Robert Browning described it poignantly in "Christmas Eve":

> . . . With arms wide open to embrace
> The entry of the human race. . . .

Tour guides, in a babel of languages, give impromptu lectures on the dimensions of the piazza; on the hundred and forty marble saints looking down at them from atop the colonnade; on the twin fountains; and on the Egyptian obelisk that climbs into the Roman skies, crowned with a bronze cross that contains a sliver of the True Cross and an inscription on the base that says it all: *Christus vincit. Christus regnat. Christus imperat.*

Originally erected at Heliopolis by the Egyptian King Nuncores, the obelisk was brought to Rome by the Emperor Caligula (37-41) and set up on the *spina*, the dividing island of his circus or racetrack in the Vatican Meadows. The track was later renamed for Emperor Nero. There the obelisk was the mute spectator of the games of the pagans and the slaughter of the Christians. Pope Sixtus V had it moved about a hundred meters or so to its present site in 1586, under the supervision of Domenico Fontana. Here it continues to be a silent spectator to the torrent of pilgrims that pours through the square every day of the year to venerate the tomb of Saint Peter.

The guides next direct their groups' attention to the great church; to the immense dome floating high above it; to the travertine front created by Stefano Maderno; to the nineteen-foot-high effigies of Christ, John the Baptist, and eleven of the apostles on the balustrade. Just before entering, the eager travelers will see what the Latin inscription on the entablature proclaims: *IN HONOREM PRINCIPIS APOSTOLORUM. PAULUS.V.BURGHESIUS ROMANUS.PONT.MAX.AN. MDCXII. PONT VII* ([This basilica] in honor of the Prince of the Apostles [was completed by] Paul V of the Roman Borghese family, Supreme Pontiff, in 1612, in the seventh year of his pontificate.) Above the central entrance is the loggia from which a newly elected pontiff imparts his first blessing, "*Urbi et Orbi.*"

The Vestibule and Interior

It has been said that despite its enormity, St. Peter's Basilica does not immediately strike the beholder as being very large. This is because everything in it is in perfect harmony. When one realizes, however, that the vestibule of St. Peter's alone is larger in area than most of the great cathedrals in the world, one begins to see things differently. At both ends of the vestibule are equestrian statues of the two great benefactors of the church—Charlemagne, to the left, and Constantine, to the right. Over the main door leading into the basilica proper is a relief of Christ entrusting the keys to Peter.

There are five doors leading from the vestibule into the basilica, of which the last on the right is the *Porta Sancta*, or Holy Door, which is open only during an *Annus Sanctus*, a Holy Year. The middle door, a masterpiece in bronze by Filarete, is composed of six panels representing the Savior, the Virgin, St. Peter, St. Paul, the beheading of Paul and the crucifixion of Peter.

Just inside and to the right is the chapel containing Michelangelo's sublime *Pieta*. Almost two hundred yards ahead, near the end of the nave, stands the main altar, and rising ten stories over it the baldachino of twisted bronze columns by Bernini. High above this is the dome, bearing on a band around its base the words of Christ to Simon Bar Jonah: *TU ES PETRUS ET SUPER HANC PETRAM AEDIFICABO MEAM ECCLESIAM ET TIBI DABO CLAVES REGNI COELORUM* (You are a Rock and upon this rock I shall build my church and I shall give unto you the Keys of the Kingdom of Heaven).

Before the altar is a sunken area, enclosed by a marble balustrade, called the *confessio*. This was an architectural feature of early Christian churches where the faithful would kneel to confess their faith in Christ Jesus. Down in this well is a marble likeness of Pope Pius VI (by Canova) absorbed in prayer, facing the crypt of St. Peter. Lining the top of the railing are nearly a hundred votive lamps which burn continuously in honor of the prince of the Apostles.

Supporting the mighty dome are four pilasters adorned with niches occupied by statues of St. Longinus, St. Helena, St. Veronica and St. Andrew. Since the pontificate of Urban VIII, these pillars have served as repositories of the four great relics housed in St. Peter's: Veronica's veil, the lance used to pierce the side of Christ, the head of St. Andrew, and a piece of the True Cross. St. Andrew of Crete informs us that the Holy Lance was found near the True Cross by Helena. St. Gregory of Tours speaks of it being venerated in the sixth century as one of the most precious relics in Christendom.

Borromini, the brilliant architect of the Baroque period, wished to dramatize the grandeur and magnitude of the Vatican Basilica. "Give me just the area of one of these pilasters and I shall create a sizable church," he said to the pope. Over on the Via delle Quattro Fontane one may see the result of this proposal: the church of San Carlo built to the precise dimensions of merely one pilaster of St. Peter's.

Just to the right of the high altar is the celebrated bronze statue of St. Peter, the left hand clutching the keys, the right hand raised in blessing. The right foot extends beyond the pedestal and has been worn smooth by the long-standing pilgrims' custom of kissing or touching it.

In the center of the apse four bronze statues of saints Ambrose, Augustine, Athanasius and John Chrysostom support the *cathedra* (chair), an ornate work by Bernini that contains the *sedia lignea*—the actual wooden chair which, according to tradition, St. Peter used.

Apart from the papal altar there are twenty-seven side altars and chapels, the most important of which is the Chapel of the Blessed Sacrament where the Eucharist is always present in the imposing tabernacle. The walls of St. Peter's are richly bedecked with monuments to numerous popes, likenesses of many founders of religious orders, mosaics and sculptured works of every description.

Music lovers might wish to pause for a moment at the tomb of Palestrina in the left transept near the entrance to the sacristy. Palestrina (1525-94) was for many years director of liturgical music at St. Peter's. Pope Pius IV compared one of the composer's masses to the music heard in heaven. Nearby, fittingly, is the tomb of Pope St. Pius X who died in 1914. Alarmed at the state of church music in his day, Pius decreed that the Roman Catholic Church should return to the Gregorian chant, or plainsong, which in his view offered a greater sense of the sacred.

More than a century in the building, St. Peter's is one of the wonders of the modern world. All of its artistic treasures notwithstanding, the most significant feature of the church remains its immensity—a total area of six acres, an external length of seven hundred feet and an internal width of four hundred and fifty feet across the transepts. From the pavement to the tip of the cross atop the dome is a distance of four hundred and sixty feet. Perhaps the most staggering statistic of all, however, is that a throng of eighty thousand can attend mass within its walls.

The *cupola*, or dome, is the world's most glorious, a miracle of art and beauty which has been built with great skill and lavished with precious materials. It is Michelangelo's architectural *magnum opus*, to which he devoted much of the last sixteen years of his life. It is the most audacious structural enterprise ever attempted. The diameter of the dome is 142 feet, just short of that of the Pantheon. Its summit is four hundred and fifty feet above the pavement of St. Peter's Square.

The least esthetic and artistic objects in St. Peter's are the humble wooden confessionals that occupy the left transept. But they dramatize most eloquently the universality of the church. Signs posted on them inform the faithful that confessions are heard here in many of the world's most prominent languages. One need not notice the confessionals, though, in order to come to the realization of such universality. On any given day, one need only look around to see that followers of Christ have flooded into St. Peter's from every nation of every continent on our planet. It is thus quite fair to call this great church the Capitol of Christendom.

Musei Vaticani

The plural *musei* is appropriate, for this is indeed an amalgamation of numerous museums, established at different times and having different focuses.

As art and antiquities displays accessible to the public, the papal museums and galleries were initiated by Clement XIV (1769-1774) and developed under his successor, Pius VI (1775-1799). Thus when the facility first opened it bore the name *Il Museo Pio-Clementino*. Pius VII (1800-1823) expanded the museum considerably, adding a wing called *Museo Chiaramonti* (his family name).

Gregory XVI (1831-1846) established an Etruscan wing for artifacts uncovered in excavations in Tuscany (in ancient times called *Etruria*). He also began a collection of Egyptian artworks and another of statues, reliefs, and mosaics from the Roman period. The Vatican Museums also include the Hall of Tapestries. The most renowned works here are those executed by Raphael and his students, portraying scenes from the life of Christ from the Nativity to the Resurrection. There is also the Gallery of Maps—huge wall paintings of each of the regions of Italy. Other attractions are the Rooms and Loggia of Raphael, featuring frescoes by the young master from Urbino; the Hall of Modern Paintings; and the *Pinacoteca*, a separate pink-brick building that houses the masterpieces of most of the prominent Renaissance artists.

Biblioteca Vaticana

Toward the end of a visit to the Vatican Museums one passes through a few rooms of the Vatican Library. The first papal library was established by Pope Saint Hilary (461-467). Wishing to make available for scholars his collection of several hundred ancient manuscripts, he set aside a few chambers in the Lateran Palace for this purpose.

In the course of the following centuries, this collection was steadily enlarged and enriched by the contributions of many popes and cardinals. When Clement V departed for Avignon in 1308, he had the entire collection transferred there. In 1447 the papal library was ordered returned to Rome by Martin V, who decided to house it thenceforth in the Vatican. Nicholas V seems to have been the founder of the present library whose vast collection of volumes and documents continues to be augmented to the present day.

The Vatican Library consists of a gallery, 1,250 feet long, divided into many sections or chambers. Walls are decorated with frescoes representing events in the pontificates of Paul V, Pius VI and Pius VII. The reading and research rooms where scholars work are on the floor below.

La Cappella Sistina

Signs bearing these three words point the way in the streets as one comes over the Tiber from the heart of Rome. A visit to the Sistine Chapel is the highlight of a tour of the Vatican Museums. The Sistine is the official private chapel of the popes and is dedicated to Our Lady Assumed into Heaven.

While there is hardly a person alive who does not know of the Sistine Chapel and its frescoes, perhaps a few details here will still be helpful to the pilgrim of A.D. 2000. Built by Sixtus IV in 1473, and named for him (there is no *x* in the Italian alphabet), the chapel was designed by two architects, Giovanni Dolci and Baccio Pintelli. Sixtus and his successors obtained the services of the most renowned Italian painters of the day for the interior decoration. The lower walls—one painted with events from the New Testament and the life of Christ, the other with scenes from the Old Testament and the life of Moses—are the collective efforts of Signorelli, Botticelli, Ghirlandaio, Pinturicchio, Rosselli and Perugino.

In 1508, Pope Julius II assigned a reluctant Michelangelo to adorn the vault of the chapel with frescoes. For his subject, Michelangelo chose the Creation and the subsequent preparation of all the world for the coming of the Messiah. He divided the surface into nine sections. In the first he portrayed God Almighty extending his arms to separate light from darkness. In the next panel he showed God creating two huge lamps, the Sun and the Moon, the first to light the world by day, the second and smaller one by night. In the subsequent three panels he depicted God creating the animals, and Man and Woman. The sixth section of the ceiling shows the Fall and the expulsion from Paradise.

The last three scenes Michelangelo devoted to Noah: surrounded by his family and offering sacrifice, the Flood, the drunkenness of Noah. All of this Michelangelo surrounded with lunettes of colossal figures of prophets and sybils. The vault was completed in 1512.

In 1535 Pope Paul III invited Michelangelo to paint the wall behind the altar. By then in his sixties, the Florentine master set to work to portray the end of the world, the antithesis of the subject he had chosen for the vault.

His *Last Judgment* shows Christ at the top, sitting as judge in the act of condemning the wicked to the fires of hell. The faces of the damned are contorted in dread, while those of the saved manifest inexpressible joy. Christ is surrounded by his mother, the apostles, and saints. Above Christ are angels bearing the symbols of his passion in triumph. Below him, a band of angels sound their trumpets in a deafening blast signaling the end of the material realm. Several skeletons struggle to resume their bodies, some toil at removing the earth that covers them, others rise in the air to the Seat of Judgment. All about, angels aid the elect in their ascent to heaven while demons and Charon the boatman drag the condemned to the inferno. The effect of the whole is indeed wondrous if apocalyptic to behold. Writers often use "terrifying beauty" to describe Michelangelo's *Last Judgment.*

Of course, the Sistine Chapel is also renowned as the world's most extraordinary polling booth. It is here, in the much ornamented chamber, that the cardinals gather to choose a successor to

Saint Peter. Following a papal election here, the College of Cardinals escort the new pontiff to the central loggia of St. Peter's Basilica where he will be introduced to the world. *Habemus Papam!* "We have a Pope!" proclaims the Dean of the Sacred College as he presents the new Bishop of Rome to the city and to the world.

The Grottoes Beneath
St. Peter's

When the new St. Peter's was built, its floor stood about three meters above that of the ancient basilica commissioned by Constantine. In the space between, Pope Gregory XIII laid out a series of grottoes to house the tombs of pontiffs that had stood in, under or near the first St. Peter's Church.

To enter this papal burial ground from the basilica, one descends a narrow spiral staircase to the left of the pilaster of Saint Longinus. (Look for a sign indicating *Tombe dei Papi*.) After following a curving corridor flanked by endless chapels, one soon comes out into three wide naves with cross-vaulted ceilings.

Down here in these hushed vaults, one feels in close contact with the earliest centuries of the church. On some of the sarcophagi, reliefs of pagan cupids merge with those of Christian cherubs. One sees the Rome of the Caesars giving way to the Rome of the Popes. Here can be found the final resting places of such successors of Peter as Boniface VIII, Nicholas III, Gregory V and Innocent X, along with names quickly recognizable to those of us of middle age and beyond, such as Benedict XV, Pius XI, Pius XII, John XXIII, Paul VI and John Paul I. It has been said that all but about ninety of the church's two hundred and sixty-four Supreme Pontiffs lie in eternal repose somewhere in the basilica, the grottoes, or in the very soil of the Vatican.

The *Scavi* (Excavations)

When Pope Pius XI died in 1939, having often expressed a wish to be buried in the Vatican Grottoes, workmen set about exploring the crypt for a suitable position for his tomb. In the course of their work, they unearthed sections of the ancient pagan cemetery over which Constantine raised the first St. Peter's Basilica. The new pope, Pius XII, gave orders for extensive excavations. Ten years of difficult digging brought the workers down into a whole street of beautifully decorated *mausolea*, a street unseen for more than sixteen centuries. The discovery was electrifying and spurred a new quest by the church to find the bones of St. Peter. A team of archeologists from the University of Rome, led by Professor Margherita Guarducci, conducted the search which two decades later led to the discovery of the human remains believed to be those of the Fisherman from Galilee. In the chest containing the bones were found some handfuls of dirt and tatters of purple and gold cloth, indicating a person of high office. This, plus graffiti marking the niche that held the chest, plus what ancient documents and tradition say about the burial of Peter, and scientific tests showing the bones to be those of a man between sixty and seventy years of age, all added up to one irrefutable conclusion as far as Professor Guarducci was concerned: Here indeed were the mortal remains of Peter the Apostle!

Pope Paul VI found the evidence persuasive enough to proclaim, in a solemn ceremony in the basilica on June 26, 1968, that centuries of tradition had been verified: St. Peter does in fact lie in eternal repose far below the great dome bearing the words that began the church: *TU ES PETRUS.*

Close about the Apostle's tomb are believed to be the bodies of his earliest successors as well, including saints Linus, Cletus, Evaristus, Sixtus, Telesphorus, Hyginus, Pius, Eleutheris and Victor—all martyred for the faith. Guided tours of these excavations are available but only through application—well in advance—to the Ufficio degli Scavi, Vatican City, 00120 Italy.

The Unknown Vatican

To most visitors the word *Vatican* represents St. Peter's Basilica, the Sistine Chapel and the various museums. But the Vatican comprises more than these.

In the paragraphs to follow, we would like to escort the reader on a walking tour of Vatican City: a miniature country completely walled-in and surrounded by a foreign city. Recognized by Italy since the Lateran Treaty of 1929 as an autonomous, sovereign state, Vatican City has its own army, postal system, currency, flag, national anthem and head of state (the pope). As mentioned earlier, this golf course-sized nation has diplomatic ties with more than a hundred others, including the United States. When we cross over the border from the capital of Italy into the Vatican, through the Saint Anne Gate, we enter into a land unique in a myriad of ways. Here is a place with no mountains, no lakes, no forests, not a single river. Here is a country with no highways, bridges or tunnels, and hence no infrastructure headaches. Here is a land with no taxes, no unemployment, no poverty, no crime, where no movie theater or restaurant or drive-through bank is to be found. Here, early each morning, children can be seen streaming across the frontier en route to school in a foreign country. The Vatican is a land with a population of less than a thousand, a world of biscuit-colored buildings and a brightly-uniformed army.

We embark on our cross-country stroll by passing through the iron *Porta Sant'Anna*, just one block beyond the right colonnade of St. Peter's Square. Here our credentials, and our purpose, will be checked by a pair of guards.

Just inside the gate and to the right is *La Chiesa Sant Anna*, the small parish church of the people who reside within the soaring eighth-century walls of Pope Leo IV. Here—not in the baroque immensity and majesty of St. Peter's—is where the *Cives Vaticani* hold their funerals. Here, each Sunday, is where they hear a sermon and drop lire into the collection basket.

Directly across the narrow street are the barracks and canteen of the little army that defends the one-hundred-and-eight-acre enclave, the Swiss Guard. A few yards further up the street and to the right begins the *Via del Pellegrino*. Along this narrow, winding street we find, beyond the parish house on the right, the central power plant, the tapestry workshop run by Franciscan sisters, the seldom-used, chapel-sized church of San Pellegrino, the offices of the state newspaper *Osservatore Romano*, and the quarters of the *Vigilanza Vaticana* (the tiny territory's law enforcement agency).

A short flight of stone steps and a hairpin turn to the left puts us on the *Via della Tipografia* that leads into the heart of village life in Vatican City, where, in the midst of Renaissance splendor and papal pageantry, the citizens lead their ordinary existence. Named for the huge printing plant of the Vatican Polyglot Press at the far end, this street brings us past the bustling pharmacy and busy post office to the *Annona*, or supermarket. The hub of neighborhood life, the *Annona* (Latin for *provisions*) opens each day at seven. By late morning, people from all walks of Vatican life have passed through and made their purchases.

Restricted to Vatican residents and workers, the market is actually a series of shops under a single roof. One sells fresh milk; another offers the best of Italian cheeses, olive oil, veal, sausage and prosciutto. The grocery division stocks spaghetti, noodles, bread, rolls, jams and canned goods. At the liquor store can be found brandies, wines, and beers from around the globe. Prices here are less than half of what they are out in the shops of Rome. So are the prices at the Vatican gasoline pumps, one of the numerous compensations for the modest salaries paid for most jobs.

And what jobs are there? Aside from the clergy who serve in the various congregations of the pope's Curia or cabinet, there are, among the citizenry, gardeners, janitors, maintenance men, mechanics, firemen, sanitation workers, laundresses, housekeepers, cooks and the fabled *San Pietrini*, the "little Saint Peters." Working out of a bureau with the enchanting name of *Reverenda Fabbrica della*

Basilica San Pietro, the *San Pietrini*—a couple of hundred strong—are responsible for keeping the venerable basilica in good physical condition, inside and out. Do not be surprised to see a squad of them, on a sunny day, swinging precariously from sixty-foot ropes, inspecting the structure, or even the dome, looking for cracks in the marble or for troublesome weeds taking root in the mortar. There are also a few orders of nuns who run the bookstore, the religious articles shop, and the hospices of this tiny country.

From the Annona, the Via Tipografia runs down to the Via del Belvedere. After a right turn here, we begin the ascent of Vatican Hill. The towering walls off to our left form the back of the Courtyard of Saint Damasus, which leads to the papal apartments high above us.

The street ends at a lofty stone gateway into whose frieze are embedded seven-foot-tall bronze letters spelling out PONT MAX, short for Pontifex Maximus, one of the Holy Father's numerous titles. Above these, a large engraved marble plaque proclaims in Latin that this gate was erected by Pope Pius XI to provide a passageway to the Vatican Library and Archives. Beyond the gate, the vastness of *Il Cortile Belvedere*, one of the Vatican's many large courtyards, spreads out before us. Its centerpiece is a large but graceful fountain, throwing forth jets of silvery water into an enormous basin.

Guards on duty here are accustomed to watching the world pass through—from cars with S.C.V. (Stato della Citta del Vaticano) license plates bringing cardinals to conferences in the Apostolic Palace; to limousines bearing world leaders to a private audience with the Holy Father; to a delegation of African envoys or a group of Shinto priests from Japan making their way on foot to the pope's offices; to the daily stream of bishops paying their obligatory quintennial visit *ad limina apostolorum*. If we follow this trail of visitors up the ramp on the far side of the court, it will bring us out into the sun-dappled bright greenery of the Vatican Gardens.

Resuming our trek, we might ponder for a moment the contrast between this edenic spot and the noisy frenetic pace of twentieth-century life pulsating just over the walls, down in the streets of Eternal Rome. All that breaks the sweet stillness and silence here, however, are birdsong, splashing fountains, murmuring evergreens, whispered conversations and the bells of St. Peter's.

Here each afternoon the pope meditates amid the countless boxwood nooks and marble busts, the shady recesses and terracotta urns, and the zigzagging pebble paths that end at an ancient statue or babbling fountain. We come now to the far right end of the gardens anchored by an exquisite pink brick palace, the *Pinacoteca*. This, the Vatican's major art gallery, boasts an array of original Michelangelos, Peruginos, Titians, Giottos and Raphaels.

From here we go left onto the *Viale della Zitella* and left again down a hedge-flanked lane, a hundred yards or so, to a dramatic statue of St. Peter rising out of its own circular grassy island. The Prince of the Apostles is shown gazing up at the great dome while clutching the keys to the kingdom of heaven. Behind the bearded fisherman roars the rugged Fountain of the Eagle. The path behind the fountain climbs through verdant lawns toward the summit of Vatican Hill. Along the way, the melodies of the Fountains of the Woods and those named for Benedict XV and Pius XI are carried on the breezes.

At the top of Vatican Hill we come to a lovely shrine to Our Lady called *La Madonna della Guardia*. Heading west through an ornamental gateway to *Fontana Rotonda*, we soon arrive at a black-topped piazza at the end of which rises a grotto, a perfect replica of the site in Lourdes, France, where the Blessed Mother appeared to Bernadette. Three slate steps lead from the center of the square up to the marvelously symmetrical Garden of the Roses featuring twin dolphin fountains and several arbors, each of which frames the dome of the basilica in the distance.

Back to the grotto we now go for a brief prayer, and then along its left wall in the direction of the antenna of *Radio Vaticana*. Turning with the narrow lane, in a minute or two we reach the Marconi Radio Station and, a little further on, the Ethiopian College, a seminary that trains future bishops for the continent of Africa. We now find ourselves on *Viale del Seminario Ethiopico* which plunges down the flank of Vatican Hill, passes under a viaduct, and comes out along the railroad tracks. The Vatican rail system is the shortest in the world—two sets of tracks about three hundred yards long that exit through a pair of massive sliding iron doors. On the other side they link up with the main Italian line, which connects with the rails of every country bordering Italy to the north.

At the bottom of the avenue and to the right reposes the white marble bulk of the Vatican Railroad Station. Elegant in its simplicity of design, the station struck the writer H. G. Morton as looking "more like a branch of the Barclay Bank in London." Across the *Piazza della Stazione* is the renowned Mosaic Studio. A customer may order a small mosaic reproduction of a famous painting. One of the craftsman will work on it and have it ready in a few weeks. The work is carried out with wonderful painstaking skill, partly due to the incredible tile stock of 28,000 tints available to the craftsmen. Off on the left, just a stone's throw, is the four-story *Governatorato*, a peach-colored Renaissance palace housing the civilian administration for the sovereign state. Here are issued passports, license plates, housing assignments, work permits and such. Fronting the building is a strikingly beautiful lawn landscaped with the papal emblems of a tiara and crossed keys.

Heading down the home stretch, now we proceed toward the back of St. Peter's Basilica, which stands there like a mountain of travertine. Down yet another stone stairway we come upon one of the tiniest churches on earth, standing within the very shadow of the largest, old *Santo Stefano degli Abessini*. Built by Leo III (795–816) it was originally known as *Santo Stefano Maggiore*. The name change came in 1479 when Sixtus IV entrusted the church to the care of Coptic monks from Abyssinia.

Our route now takes us through an archway connecting the basilica's sacristy on our left to the Hospice of Saint Marta. Directly before us looms the modern 10,000-seat audience hall from the reign of Paul VI. From here it's a short distance around twenty-foot-high brick walls, baked golden by centuries of Mediterranean sun and surmounted by a marble balustrade. These enclose a small trapezoidal plot of burial ground called the *Campo Santo Teutonico*, or German Cemetery. Tradition claims that Constantine filled this plot with soil brought back from Calvary. Around the interior walls are the Stations of the Cross in ceramic. The tombstones are works of art, the epitaphs works of literature. On the outside wall a plaque informs us that here stood the Circus of Nero where, before a howling pagan mob, Peter and great numbers of his flock shed their blood for the infant church. The area is fittingly named Piazza of the Protomartyrs.

Our imaginary border-to-border walking tour concludes as we cross over the frontier through the Porta Sant Uffizio back into sunny Italy. *Grazie della vostra compagnia.*

Note: A vicarious tour such as this must suffice for most of us. Such freedom of movement within the Vatican walls is not permitted to non-citizens. At the various gates Swiss Guards will allow you to pass if you name an office with which you have business to conduct, say for example the *Osservatore Romano,* but should you seek to wander from your destination, you will be turned away by other guards.

The Vatican Gardens

Over the steep northern and western slopes of Vatican Hill, on the left bank of the Tiber, ramble the *Giardini Vaticani*. Originating in the late Middle Ages, these fifty acres of luxuriant and richly-ornamented gardens afford the pope a tranquil, verdant setting where each day he can restore his soul after the rigors of his awesome task. Here among the fountains, trees and shady recesses, the Holy Father can meditate, contemplate or simply unwind, with the eyes of only an occasional imperial-age statue upon him.

It was under Pope Boniface VIII, at the beginning of the fourteenth century, that a modest garden of medicinal herbs was cultivated on this site. By the end of that century, due to the enthusiasm of subsequent popes, this had evolved into sprawling botanical gardens, among the most important in Europe.

In 1559, Pius IV constructed his splendid *casina*, or summer-house. This biscuit-colored stucco building in the midst of the gardens, with its delicate proportions and mosaic facing, is a precious gem in a flawless setting. Lanciani called it "a perfect image of an ancient Roman country house." The Casina is the work of the distinguished Renaissance architect, Pirro Ligorio. When Pius did not care to make the rumbling journey along the old Appian Road to his summer residence in the hill town of Castel Gandolfo, he would come down from the hot upper floors of the Apostolic Palace to spend a few days and nights in his Casina, savoring the soft air and pleasing fragrances of the Vatican Gardens. In front of the summer-house he had laid out an enclosed elliptical courtyard with built-in stone benches. This intellectual and cultivated pontiff fostered learning and liked to host convocations of the leading minds of the day in this courtyard. These sessions, called *Notti Vaticane*—Vatican Evenings—revolved around discussions of poetry, philosophy, art and theology. Later popes used to grant audiences in the Casina courtyard. In our time, this complex serves as the headquarters of the Pontifical Academy of Sciences. Pope Pius V (1566–1572), no less ardently interested in the gardens than his predecessor, called in the most gifted landscapers to develop them further. Under Alexander VII in 1655 the gardens were extended yet again, so that for a time they even spilled out beyond the walls and up the flanks of the Janiculum Hill to the ridge where the Pauline Fountain stands. Future pontiffs would embellish the gardens with buildings and fountains, pine forests and sculptured shrubbery, rock formations and cobblestone lanes.

The golden age of the Vatican Gardens came under the saintly Leo XIII in the late 1800s. Indefatigable, Leo pushed himself with incredibly long work days and monastic personal discipline. His table was frugal. His only recreation was to spend the early afternoon in the green oasis behind the basilica where he would stroll, recite his breviary, say the rosary, hum a favorite aria or simply sit in the shade of an umbrella pine. He wished the gardens to be as beautiful as possible. His gardeners put in long narrow lanes, flanked by myrtle and boxwood trees, which provided a poetic, bucolic ambience.

The Catholic people of France contributed to the beautification project, donating to His Holiness a replica of the grotto at Lourdes. A blue-gowned statue of the Blessed Virgin stands near the entrance to the cave where the miraculous spring of Bernadette is symbolized by three jets of water cascading over the rocks. A marble plaque bears this exhortation: *"Allez boire a la fontaine et vous laver"* — "Go drink at the fountain and cleanse yourself." The grotto quickly became a favorite stop in Leo's daily stroll.

Knowing of Leo XIII's love for creatures, in 1888 the bishop of Carthage gave the bishop of Rome a miniature zoo, with an enormous aviary and enclosures of deer, goats, ostriches, and the like. Leo developed a special fondness for the gazelles and seemed to linger a bit longer at their area. On a languid autumn afternoon in 1889 one of these graceful animals broke loose, leaped upon Leo XIII and began to lick his face. A Vatican guard walking nearby feared for the Holy Father's life. The amused pope, however, quickly calmed the playful gazelle and reassured the worried gendarme. Afterwards the wry old man could not resist having some fun with the guard. "Did you really think that a gazelle could defeat a lion?" the pope asked with a grin. (Leo's name in Italian—*Leone*—means "lion.") The pope also had a pet cat that made its home in the gardens and with whom he would share his daily dish of *polenta*. Not long afterward, "Papa Pecci," as the Romans knew him, had constructed in a shady nook of the gardens a charming kiosk where he would take his afternoon espresso. The workers on the grounds named the tiny structure "Coffee House." Around this time Pope Leo fashioned a summer retreat out of one of the towers in the ninth-century walls that encircle Vatican City.

In his final months the ailing Leo XIII, too weak to walk his beloved gardens, used to tour them by horse and carriage. Every now and then he would have the driver stop at a favorite spot. Then, while sipping a glass of watered-down claret, he would reflect on his long life and his long pontificate, and ponder the world beyond. For such inward journeys the Vatican Gardens were ideal and idyllic.

Here at morning and eventide one is treated to the most enchanting music—the song of the birds, the bells of St. Peter's, the murmuring waters of the fountains. One walks down lanes lined with laurel, cypress and pine, lanes that pleasantly cross and recross one another. One treks up and down rolling hills that are profuse with stone and vegetation. One catches glimpses of shady recesses and boxwood nooks, of lonely imperial statues and busts, of sarcophagi ornamented with bas reliefs of flute-playing youths staring out here and there from some leafy thicket, of romantic urns and columns without number—all arousing vague dreams of those long ago Edens of Imperial Rome's aristocracy, stirring strange sensations of déjà vu. One delights in the smells of fruit and of blossoms. First this vignette, then another beckons you. There's the majestic and roaring Fountain of the Eagle; there's the garden centerpiece—a fishpond embraced by twin archways of clipped ilex that from various angles frame the dome of St. Peter's; there's the dramatic statue of the Fisherman from Galilee facing his great church. How Papa Pecci loved this place!

The death of the aged Leo XIII in 1903 ushered in a decade of decline for the Vatican Gardens. His successor, Pius X, took little or no interest in them, and they fell into neglect. But when Benedict XV ascended the Chair of Peter in 1914, he brought with him a zest for *la passeggiata*—the stroll. Again the gardens came into prominence in this miniature country—the Country of the Spirit, as one writer has called it.

Benedict took a deep interest in the gardens. He would walk through them regularly, complimenting and encouraging the groundskeepers in their efforts to nurture all the vegetation back to robust health. His successor, Pius XI, avidly supported the restoration work, even installing fifty miles of pipeline so that all the greenery could be properly irrigated, especially in the hot, dry Roman summer. The animal pens were by this time unoccupied except for a solitary eagle, a gift of an anonymous donor to Pius XI to honor his earlier achievements as a mountain climber. During this time the twin transmitting towers of Vatican Radio were erected, incongruous steel sculptures in these Renaissance gardens.

When Eugenio Pacelli ascended the throne of Peter as Pope Pius XII, he made an afternoon walk in the gardens an invariable part of his daily regimen, rain or shine. When he grew frail in his last few years, Pius's doctors pressured him to discontinue the walks in bad weather. But Pius would not hear of it. To a portion of the ancient walls he had an overhang attached so that even in the worst *Tramontana* (or Alpine rainstorm) he could still enjoy his afternoon garden interlude.

Rotund Pope John XXIII used to walk off his midday meal in the gardens without fail each day. Incurably gregarious, John liked to make small talk with the workers he met along the way. "This looks like thirsty work," he often remarked to them and would order a decanter of chilled Frascati and some glasses to be brought from the papal kitchen. When the *vino* arrived, the pontiff and the workmen would sit together on a bench or on a low retaining wall and chat. Pope John also refurbished Leo XIII's summer house in the tower with the intention of spending the months of July and August in it. Word soon reached him, however, that the local economy of

Castel Gandolfo depended on the hordes of pilgrims that came each summer to see the pope. With some disappointment, Papa Roncalli abandoned his plan for the tower.

Pope Paul VI and his successor John Paul I put the gardens to daily use as well. John Paul II also loves the grounds and often invites members of the Curia to walk with him there to discuss, in this ambience of serene loveliness, pressing matters of the universal church. According to friends of mine in the Swiss Guard, he was often spotted, early in his pontificate, outfitted in gym clothes, jogging down the shady lanes.

Here in these magnificent gardens, bejeweled with marble, popes have for centuries found peace of mind, soul and body. Here they have managed to reinvigorate themselves for their demanding mission of carrying out the work of the Prince of Peace. The Vatican Gardens, it would seem, are an important section of the vineyards of the Lord.

St. John Lateran–Cathedral of the Diocese of Rome

*O*mnium Ecclesiarum Urbis et Orbis Mater et Caput, reads the inscription at the entrance. (Of all the churches in the city and in the world this is the mother and head.) We are at the threshold of the Christian world as we read these words. We are at the doors to the Church of St. John Lateran in Rome.

This sacred building was the first great Christian church ever built, its construction taking place even before the echo of the momentous edict of A.D. 313 had faded. The ancient basilica was raised on the Lateran property in the southwest corner of the city by order of the Emperor Constantine, who named it in honor of Our Lord: *Basilica Salvatoris.* In the time of Nero, Plautus Lateranus was a leading member of Roman society and an extensive landholder. Caught in an assassination plot against the demented ruler, he was executed, his land confiscated and declared state property. After ending the persecutions, Constantine gave this property to the Christian community for the purpose of erecting there a temple for public worship. He also commissioned the building of an adjacent palace to serve as the papal residence.

Over the succeeding centuries a number of fires and earthquakes threatened the Constantinian structure with collapse, forcing Pope Sergius III in 904 to completely rebuild it. The work finished, Sergius added a dedication to St. John the Baptist to the name of the church. Two centuries later Pope Lucius included St. John the Evangelist as a second patron for the basilica. Ever since, the church has been known as *San Giovanni in Laterano,* St. John Lateran.

After two-and-a-half centuries of existence as a forbidden cult, as a literally underground church whose sacred mysteries had to be

Church of St. John at the Latin Gate/San Giovanni in Laterano

celebrated in catacombs, the Christian community in Rome had to make the pleasant adjustment upward. Now the prayers of the mass resounded through the vast cathedral commissioned by the state authorities. No longer was the bishop of Rome public enemy number one. He lived thereafter in a palace, appearing in public to impart his apostolic blessing on and receive the acclamation of the Roman throng. As the diocesan cathedral of Rome, St. John's enjoyed, and still enjoys, preeminence over all other churches, even St. Peter's. The entire site was referred to by the local flock simply as *Il Laterano*, the Lateran, in much the same way as we today refer to the Petrine basilica, the adjoining palace, and the surrounding grounds as *Il Vaticano*, the Vatican. Perhaps it is difficult to imagine the Lateran as having the same aura, the same prestige, the same significance as that associated with the Vatican. But that's precisely the way things were for a thousand years, from the pontificate of

Miltiades in the early 300s to the reign of Benedict XI in the early 1300s.

When in 1377 Gregory XI brought the seat of the papacy from Avignon back to Rome, instead of going to the Lateran with all its bad memories, he continued on the Aurelian Way to the Vatican, which a few centuries earlier had been fortified by Pope Leo IV with impregnable walls. Here the successor to Peter and the Holy See would be far safer. The prestige of the Lateran was henceforth eclipsed by that of the Vatican as the seat of papal power.

The grandeur of St. Peter's nothwithstanding, the Lateran church remains to this day the pope's official church, his diocesan cathedral, in his primary role as the local bishop. This is attested to

Saint John at the Latin Gate

by the traditional solemn ceremony, a few days after his election, in which a new pope goes in formal procession to claim St. John's as his church. Papal funeral rites also bear witness to the preeminence of the Lateran church. When Pope Paul VI's remains were brought back from Castel Gandolfo to Rome to lie in state in St. Peter's, the cortege first paused at St. John's.

The current appearance of the Basilica of San Giovanni is the work of Antonio Galilei, who fashioned the immense and dramatic baroque exterior in observance of the Holy Year of 1750. Like St. Peter's and all other Constantinian churches—such as St. Paul's, St. Lawrence's and St. Agnes (all outside the walls of Rome)—St. John's faces the rising sun. Galilei's double arcade of five openings, with a central loggia on the upper level, is resplendent in the morning light. Crowning the front entrance are nineteen-foot-high statues of Christ and his apostles, their outlines visible from all points of the city and even beyond. "The saints live in our very skies," Romans like to boast. Upon entering the Lateran we pass through an elegant atrium, on the left end of which is an equestrian statue of the church's builder and benefactor, Constantine. The two noble central doors before us are generally closed. These tall, dense, bronze portals with their beautiful patina come from the Roman Forum where for centuries they opened onto the Senate Chamber. Through them passed, on many occasions, Caesar, Cicero, Brutus, Cassius, Crassus, Augustus, Mark Anthony and Vespasian, a *Who's Who* of Roman history. After the fall of the imperial capital, the doors were taken to the Lateran to adorn the great church. To the extreme right is the *Porta Sancta*, or holy door, opened only to mark a Jubilee Year.

Borromini is responsible for the present interior. By authorization of Innocent X in 1650, he laid out five naves separated by four rows of pilasters that conceal previous supporting columns. The pilasters are fluted and of composite (Ionic and Corinthian) orders. The large niche in each of these supporting posts—facing the center aisle—contains a colossal statue (15 feet tall) of an apostle, the work of Borromini's students. Above these effigies are excellent bas reliefs in stucco. Borromini brings all this—arches, pilasters, columns, reliefs, statues—along with the Cosmati pavement of two centuries earlier—into a marvelous orchestration of elements. As a result, this immense, richly-ornamented hall is a study in spectacular harmony.

The main altar has below it a confessio, before which lies the tomb of Pope Martin V (1417–1431). Over the altar rises Arnolfo di Cambio's magnificent thirteenth-century Gothic canopy, and above this a reliquary that is said to contain the heads of the Apostles Peter and Paul. Housed within the altar is another precious relic—the wooden portable altar said to have been used by Peter himself. The apse in which the altar is set is itself a work of art, with its mosaic of the Redeemer.

Leo XIII, the pope who brought the church into the twentieth century, so loved the Lateran Basilica that he selected it as his final resting place. His tomb is in the left transept. At the end of this transept is a door leading to the medieval cloister. This outdoor retreat of peace and piety once formed part of the monastery established at St. John's by the Benedictines of Monte Cassino in the sixth century. With its alternating straight and twisted columns, its tiled rooftop and its walls embedded with fragmented antiquities, this place is a paradigm of Romanesque cloister architecture.

The right transept leads into Piazza San Giovanni, in the center of which stands the highest and most ancient of Rome's twelve obelisks. The fifteenth century B.C. monolith once graced the Temple of the Sun in Heliopolis. Its original position in Rome was on the *spina*, or dividing island, of the Circus Maximus. When the Renaissance pope, Sixtus V, embellished the northern entrance of St. John's, he brought the obelisk here to the piazza. On the right edge of the busy square is the octagonal baptistry, the church's first structure built expressly for the administration of the sacrament. One tradition says that Constantine ordered its construction over the site where he himself was baptized by Pope Sylvester I. Eusebius, however, relates in his history of the church that Constantine received the sacrament on his deathbed.

Exiting San Giovanni in Laterano from the front, one is treated to a sweeping vista. Diagonally to the left is the shrine built by

Domenico Fontana in 1586 to house the *Scala Santa*. This is the staircase of twenty-eight steps that once was part of the palace of Pontius Pilate. It has long been held that Christ climbed these steps when he was brought before Pilate. The Empress Saint Helena, mother of Constantine, had them dismantled and brought to Rome for public veneration.

Here from the top of the front steps of St. John's one looks out over a pastoral scene, a sleepy little park. Across the piazza is the monument to St. Francis and his friars. At the end of the tree-flanked *Via Carlo Felice* six blocks away is the impressive Church of Santa Croce in Gerusalemme, and in the distance, a low line of purple mountains, the Alban Hills.

Some of my most memorable interludes in Rome have been spent on a bench in that park. In the spring, especially in May, I love to sit here in the soft warm air of early evening, listening to the song of the birds, the laughter of children, the conversation of the elderly *cives Romani*. The steady hum of the traffic, the wheeze of the green public buses, the rumble of the orange trolley cars add appealingly to the unusual sound track. At such times I love to ponder the many tiles of this exquisite mosaic—the Gate of St. John which pierces the red brick Aurelian Wall, the almond trees in blossom contrasting with the deepening green of the pines and cypresses, the rampant wisteria, the images of Christ and his apostles on high fading uncertainly into silhouettes against the flames of the western sky. In this setting, awed as I am, I grow mindful of Dante's lines from his *Divine Comedy*:

> *Se I barbari venendo da tal plaga . . .*
> *Veggendo Roma e L'ardua sua opera*
> *Stupefaciensi, quando Laterano*
> *Alle cose mortali ando di sopra . . .*
> *Di che stupor dovea esser compiuto.*

("If the barbarians from the distant land coming to Rome were astonished by her great monuments, when above all of which rose the Lateran, just imagine how moved was I.")

Saint Mary Major:
The Church of the Snows

St. Mary Major is one of the four patriarchal basilicas of Rome, the others being St. Peter's, St. John Lateran and St. Paul's Outside the Walls. Like the other three, St. Mary's dates to the first half of the fourth century. There is a charming story about its beginnings that has persisted down through the centuries. According to the legend, a wealthy citizen of Rome by the name of Ioannes Patricius, in the year 350, had prayed to the Blessed Mother to give his life more meaning. In the early morning hours of August 5, Mary appeared to Patricius in a dream, urging him to erect a church in her honor where he found snow that day in Rome. When he called on his friend Pope Liberius a few hours later, the pontiff revealed that he had had the same dream. Hardly a few minutes had passed when an aide to the Holy Father burst in with the startling news that the summit of the Esquiline Hill was under a blanket of snow. The two friends hastened to the spot, whereupon Liberius took his crosier and walked around the site, etching in the snow the outline of the huge basilica he now intended to build there with the financial support of his nobleman friend. Soon there began to rise the greatest shrine to the Mother of Jesus. In 432 Pope Sixtus III richly embellished the structure to commemorate the declaration of Mary's divine motherhood by the Council of Ephesus.

Over the centuries since, there have been numerous restorations and ornamentations. Yet in many respects, especially regarding the interior, Santa Maria Maggiore remains essentially the church that Pope Liberius built. Upon your entry into the basilica, stop for a few moments to ponder a while this striking and stately hall that spreads out before you. The thirty-six columns, hewn out of single blocks of Athenian marble, that flank the great central nave never fail to impress the visitor. Above each is a mosaic panel

Santa Maria Maggiore

with an Old Testament theme. As you move solemnly down the two-hundred-and-eighty-foot-long main aisle, you recognize, in these mosaics, scenes from the lives of Abraham, Isaac, Jacob, Esau, Moses and Joshua. From time to time, try to focus your eyes downward to appreciate the fine twelfth-century Cosmati floor of inlaid marble patterns.

In the next century the graceful apse was added. This is crowned by the masterpiece mosaic of the Franciscan friar Torriti (1295), depicting the coronation of Mary by her divine Son. In 1377 the bell tower was erected, at two hundred and fifty feet the highest of the Romanesque campaniles to punctuate the Roman skyline. The coffered ceiling is the work of Giulio Sangallo, one of the many architects who labored on the construction of St. Peter's. It is gilded with the first gold brought back from the New World by Columbus, the gift of King Ferdinand and Queen Isabella of

Spain. A few years prior to the Holy Year of 1750, Ferdinando Fuga, the Florentine, by commission of Benedict XIV, designed the exterior you see today, with five entrances (like St. Peter's), and a loggia, or balcony—for papal blessings—above them (also like the *Vatican basilica*).

Added at this time too was the *baldachino*, or canopy, over the high altar. Four porphyry columns of the Corinthian order hold the canopy aloft. The altar, of porphyry as well, is still the original one donated by Patricius and his wife to Pope Liberius. Four gilded bronze angels support a beautiful tabernacle, also of gilded bronze. In front of the altar is a deep well, the *confessio*, with twin staircases descending into it. The *confessio* is also noteworthy for the excellent kneeling sculpture of Pius IX, and for a reliquary containing what are said to be parts of the *praesepio*, or manger, used as the baby Jesus' first crib. In fact, it is this precious relic that accounts for one of the four names by which this great Marian basilica is known: *Santa Maria ad Praesepe*. The Romans also refer to this church as *Santa Maria ad Nives* (of the Snows), as the *Basilica Liberiana* (for its builder) and of course as *Santa Maria Maggiore*. In the crypt beneath the altar there is also the tomb of a martyr: St. Matthias, the apostle chosen to fill the vacancy left by Judas.

On the right end of the transept is the Chapel of the Blessed Sacrament. Built by order of Pope Sixtus V, it is also called the Sistine Chapel. (This is not to be confused with the renowned Vatican edifice, named for Sixtus IV and frescoed by Michelangelo.) The tomb of Sixtus V, that great Renaissance city planner, is to be found in this room. Entombed here as well is the Dominican pope, St. Pius V. Crowning this holy place is one of the church's twin cupolas.

The corresponding chapel on the opposite end of the transept was built in 1611 by Paul V of the distinguished Roman Borghese clan. There is much to recommend this room, not the least of which is the splendid icon of the Blessed Mother high above the main altar. Tradition claims it is the work of St. Luke. That it dates to apostolic times has been certified. Beneath the icon is the inscription honoring Mary as *Salus Populi Romani*—protectress of the

Roman people. In this chapel one sees also the monumental sepulchre of Paul V, with bas-reliefs recording the achievements of his pontificate. On the altar of this chapel, on April 3, 1899, Father Eugenio Pacelli, who grew up just blocks away, celebrated his first mass. Forty years later he was crowned in St. Peter's as Pope Pius XII.

Nathaniel Hawthorne was so taken by the beauty of this room that he was moved to write: "Unless words were gems that would flame with many coloured lights upon the page and thence throw a tremendous glimmer into the reader's eyes, it were vain to attempt a description of this princely chapel." I too love this part of Saint Mary Major's, but particularly on the fifth of August. On that day each year a special mass is celebrated here. At the consecration, thousands upon thousands of white rose petals are suddenly released from a net high up in the cupola to symbolize the legendary founding of this church. For this reason the room is called the Chapel of the Snows.

You may leave the solemn beauty of Santa Maria through the front door and step into the Piazza Santa Maria which is graced by a hundred-foot-high column, surmounted by an effigy of the Mother of Christ, or by the door to the rear of the main altar and thrill to the towering obelisk of Piazza dell'Esquilino. This massive funeral monument was brought to Rome in the fourth century from Axum, the holy city of Ethiopia.

Should you be fortunate enough to make a pilgrimage to Rome, do not fail to highlight your trip with an unhurried visit to the principal Marian church in all the world, Santa Maria Maggiore.

Basilica of St. Paul's Outside the Walls

St. Paul's Outside the Walls

Among the great Christian shrines of Rome, one of the favorites of many pilgrims—and of the Romans themselves—is a church with the rather poetic name of St. Paul's Outside the Walls. In addition to its architectural magnificence and artistic abundance, the place has a rich and interesting history that reaches back to apostolic times.

Tradition has it that the Apostle Paul was executed by decapitation in the year 67, two miles beyond the gates of Rome on the road to Ostia. (In his writings, St. Clement, the fourth pope, hints that the Emperor Nero himself was present at the grim proceedings.) Paul's body was claimed by the Roman matron Lucina, a leading member of the early Christian community in the city, who interred the holy remains nearby in her vineyard along the banks of the Tiber. About a decade later, Pope Anacletus, second successor to St. Peter, marked the grave with a small mortuary chapel. Such *memoriae* were considered inviolate by Roman law. Devout Christians would trek daily to this hallowed spot to pray at the apostle's grave, despite official Rome's ban on the practice of Christianity. In 324, after ending the persecutions and granting freedom of worship to the Christians, Constantine commissioned the building of a basilica over the tomb of Paul. Since the final resting place of the apostle was situated so close beside the main road to Ostia, it was impossible to erect a large church on such a cramped site. Furthermore, it could not be orientated toward the east as was the basilica honoring Peter over in the Vatican district.

Constantine had the chancel of his church to Paul and the arch leading into the sanctuary adorned with mosaics. The tomb itself he covered with an elaborate bronze sarcophagus. Concerning Constantine's building of monumental churches over the tombs of the apostles, the *Liber Pontificalis*, a book written in the sixth century, is very precise: *Fecit basilicam S. Paolo Apostolo cuius corpus recondidit in arca et conclusit, sicut Petri*, which means: He made a basilica for St. Paul the Apostle, whose body he put back again in a chest and sealed it, just as he had done for Peter.

And yet Constantine's effort soon proved to be insufficient. In the years that followed, the crush of Christians wanting to worship here warranted a larger edifice. Increasing throngs of pilgrims from abroad and a growing Christian community at home moved Emperor Valentinian II in 386 to raze it and build a much larger church. This wondrous shrine was to survive the ravages of time, the buffeting of storms, and the vicissitudes of history until the summer of 1823—an astounding span of 1,437 years. It was later lavishly decorated with mosaics and other adornments by Galla Placida, daughter of the emperor Honorius and wife of Adolphus, King of the Goths.

The great temple and all its treasures were spared by Alaric in his march on Rome, but suffered considerably in the Vandal sack of 455 when Genseric approached the city by the Via Ostiense. It was subsequently restored, only to suffer again at the hands of the invading Lombards in 730. Later that same century, the church of St. Paul's Outside the Walls was rebuilt by Pope Leo II. Soon afterwards, the basilica was surrounded by monastic buildings, cloisters, hospitals, baths, granaries, and ultimately by a full fledged suburb of Rome called *Johnannipolis*, since it was developed largely under Pope John VIII (872–882). In time, however, malaria took its deadly hold on the area, due to frequent flooding of the Tiber, and John VIII's once flourishing fortified village fell into ruin. When Hildebrand first came as a monk to the adjoining monastery in the eleventh century, only a few dissolute brethren remained. The district became a cow pasture. Grazing flocks would even wander into the venerable basilica from time to time.

Throughout the rest of the Middle Ages, and on into the Renaissance and the modern era, St. Paul's Outside the Walls remained a focal point of pilgrimage. In the early hours of July 15, 1823, disaster struck the ancient and holy edifice. Due to the carelessness of workmen repairing the roof—they had left burning a pan of charcoal—the tinder-dry wooden beams ignited and quickly collapsed into the nave. By dawn, the stately shrine in honor of Paul the Apostle lay in charred ruins. Only the great archway over the entrance to the sanctuary, the thirteenth-century baldachino over the main altar, the apse with its mosaic from the same period and the adjacent cloister survived the devastation. Word of the catastrophe spread rapidly through all of the city. Everyone knew about it and wept over it, except Rome's leading citizen, Pope Pius VII, who lay dying in his summer residence on the Quirinale Hill.

In his biography of this pope, Cardinal Nicholas Wiseman tells us why the news that St. Paul's had burned was kept from him:

> Not a word was said to the dying Pius VII of the destruction of St. Paul's. For at St. Paul's he had lived as a quiet monk, engaged in study and in teaching, and he loved that place with the force of an early attachment. It would have added a mental pang to his bodily sufferings to learn the total destruction of

that cherished sanctuary, in which he had drawn down by prayer the blessings of Heaven on his youthful labour.

In his fitful sleep the previous night, Pius VII had dreamed over and over again that the Roman Church was about to suffer some terrible misfortune. He died days later, unaware that his nightmare had come to pass.

Stendhal, the famous nineteenth-century writer who happened to be in Rome at the time, describes the scene for us in his *Roman Journal*:

> I visited St. Paul's on the day following the fire. I found in it a serene beauty and an impression of calamity such as only the music of Mozart, among the fine arts, can suggest. Everything conveyed the horror and disorder of the disaster; the church was cluttered with smoking and half-burnt beams; great fragments of columns split from top to bottom threatened to fall at the slightest jar. The Romans who filled the ravaged church were thunderstruck.

Rebuilding was begun at once, thanks to the generosity of the heartbroken people of Rome and of people of all faiths from around the globe. Six alabaster columns came from Mohemet Ali, viceroy of Egypt. Czar Nicholas I of Russia sent two precious malachite altars to be placed at the ends of the transept. From the rebuilding, which was finished in 1854, the basilica emerged even more beautiful and complete than before the fire, for it now had an attractive new atrium. The original had disappeared by the fourteenth century. The restorers, as faithfully as possible, had reproduced the old structure. The granite used in the reconstruction was quarried at Baveno in northern Italy, the marble at Carrara.

To enter the splendid Pauline shrine today one passes through a pillared portico and atrium, the largest in Rome. The colonnade encloses an elegant symmetrical garden where stands a powerful colossus of Paul, with the fire of God in his eyes. His broad shoulders sag from the burdens of his mission and his trials. Panels of colored Cappadocian marble highlight the lower portion of the facade. High above in the tympanum, a massive mosaic shows our Lord with saints Peter and Paul on either side. Just below them are depicted, with thousands of tiny colored tiles, the Divine Lamb and the Sheep (the faithful) coming from the mystical city of Jerusalem, representing the Jews, and from Bethlehem, symbolic of the Gentiles. The panel below this shows the prophets Isaias, Jeremias, Ezechial and Daniel. This masterpiece was done by the renowned Vatican Mosaic School, from 1854–74.

Five doors lead into the basilica, but only the central entrance, flanked by colossal statues of Peter and Paul, is in general use. The entrance to the extreme right is the *Porta Sancta*, or Holy Door. As do the other three patriarchal basilicas of Rome—St. Peter's, St. John Lateran and St. Mary Major—St. Paul's has a Holy Door which is opened by the pope at the beginning of each Holy Year.

The first impression a visitor to St. Paul's has is one of a vast dark hall. But as the eyes adjust, there is a feeling of awe as one discerns the dense forest of pillars reflected—as in a mirror—in the highly-polished marble pavement. Soft light filters through the alabaster windows high above, casting warm brown shadows.

Most of Rome's ancient basilicas consist of three aisles, but St. Paul's is a five-aisled church, which heightens the sense of vastness for the visitor. Eighty columns of granite separate the central nave from the four side aisles. Just above the columns lining the central aisle and the two aisles immediately flanking it are mosaic portraits of all the popes, from St. Peter to the present Holy Father. Legend tells us that when St. Paul's runs out of space for these papal portraits, the world will come to an end.

The coffered ceiling is richly ornamented, with the arms of Pius IX, one of the restorers of the basilica, in the center. Just before the main altar—where only the pope may celebrate mass—is the deep well of the *confessio*, so characteristic of the churches of ancient Rome. Under the floor of the *confessio* lies the body of St. Timothy, priest and martyr. Standing like sentries at either side of the staircase leading to the papal altar are two more giant effigies of Peter and Paul, a constantly recurring theme in the art and sculpture of the holy shrines of the Eternal City.

Over the altar, as of old, rises the magnificent baldachino, creation of Arnolfo di Cambio, architect of the stupendous cathedral of Santa Maria del Fiore in Florence. Directly beneath all this splendor still repose the bones of the man who had gone to Damascus as the fiercest prosecutor of the Christians, only to end up as the most zealous propagator of the faith.

The striking mosaic of the apse was begun under Innocent III (1198-1216) and completed in the pontificate of Gregory IX (1227-1241). Represented here are our Lord in the company of Peter, Paul, Luke and Andrew. At the right foot of Christ is a tiny figure, wrapped in white, representing Pope Honorius III (1216-1227). Beneath the apse is another beautifully adorned altar. In the left transept are the Altar of the Conversion, the Chapel of St. Stephen and the Blessed Sacrament Chapel. In the right transept

Saint Stephen of the Abyssinians in the Vatican

are to be found the Altar of St. Lawrence, the Altar of St. Benedict and the Lady Altar. Just beyond these are the Oratory of St. Julian and the Baptistry. To the right of the main altar is the famous paschal candlestick, carved by Nicholas de Angelo and Pietro Vassalletto in 1170, its bas-reliefs depicting scenes from the Passion of our Lord.

At the end of the right transept is a door leading into a large hall which contains an impressive statue of Gregory VI. This hall in turn leads to the beautiful cloister, one of the most serene spots in all the world, where the Benedictine monks of the monastery attached to St. Paul's still meditate each afternoon. Happily for pilgrims to Rome, the monks kindly allow public access to this cloister in the morning hours and again after the siesta.

I go out to St. Paul's Outside the Walls often, and my visit always culminates in a stop at the cloister. It is quiet here, far removed from the hurly-burly of the inner city. Yet as often as I go I still find it difficult to take my leave of this lovely spot, for the atmosphere is so conducive to prayer and piety and contemplation. As I leave, I have the haunting feeling that I am breaking up a warm conversation with my God.

Saint Lawrence Outside the Walls: The Double Church

On the ancient road to Tivoli, the Via Tiburtina, just beyond the Aurelian Walls rises one of Rome's most historic and fascinating churches—the *Basilica di San Lorenzo Fuori le Mura*, Saint Lawrence's Outside the Walls. In imperial times it stood isolated and picturesque among the groves and vineyards and meadows of the *campagna romana*. Today, almost engulfed by a modern suburb, it must be approached through a patchwork of narrow, twisting, congested streets.

As a deacon of the early church, Lawrence worked closely with the saintly Pope Sixtus II in gathering food, clothing and alms for

San Lorenzo Fuori le Mura

the poor. This took place in the middle of the third century. The historian Eusebius relates how the Emperor Valerian was at first cordial toward the Christians. Suddenly, faced with a myriad of problems across the length and breadth of the Roman Empire in 258, he launched a savage persecution of the church. For anyone found participating in Christian worship, the death penalty was carried out automatically, swiftly and violently.

On August 6 of that turbulent year, Pope Sixtus was condemned to death. Before his execution, the aged pontiff entrusted the treasury of the church to Lawrence, whom he loved like a son. The saintly deacon, his face damp with tears, asked of Sixtus: "Will you go without your son? Shall I not be at your side once more in this last sacrifice?" To which the Holy Father replied, "My son, thou shalt rejoin me in three days." Then he instructed Lawrence to sell the sacred vessels and all other material possessions of the church, and divide the proceeds among the city's poor.

The pontiff having been slain, the city prefect demanded that the deacon turn over all the treasures of the church to the *Aerarium*, the state coffers. Lawrence begged for a few days' extension of the deadline for this order. Three days later, Deacon Lawrence, trailed by a throng of tattered, sickly, starving beggars, showed up at the prefect's office. "Behold," he announced to the stern-faced official, "these are the treasures of Mother Church." Feeling he was being mocked, the prefect commanded that Lawrence should first be beaten bloody with whips and then roasted to death over a gridiron heated by red-hot coals. Pope Sixtus' prophecy proved accurate. Lawrence's remains were gathered by a group of Christians who interred them in the catacombs out on the road to Tivoli.

Constantine raised a modest church over the resting place of Deacon Lawrence. This church was enlarged and embellished under Pope Pelagius in the middle of the sixth century, and became known as *Sanctus Laurentius Extra Muros* (in Italian, *San Lorenzo Fuori le Mura*; in English, Saint Lawrence's Outside the Walls).

In the early seventh century a large church was built adjoining the back of San Lorenzo's, with the outer walls of their apses actually touching. When Honorius III was elected as a successor to

St. Peter, one of his first monumental works was to remove both apses and connect the two churches, which left the original altar now in the center of both structures—something unique in the Christian world. The front entrance was, from that point on, through the back of the "double church"—which featured a portico of six graceful Ionic columns.

That early-church architecture was influenced by the form of synagogues becomes apparent upon entering. The ancient orthodox Jewish community, for example, had upper galleries where the women would gather. Since the primitive Christian community of the city of Rome consisted largely of Jewish converts, this feature in a number of ancient churches is not very surprising.

This beloved church stood unchanged across the next eight centuries. But in 1944 it suffered devastation from Allied bombers seeking to demolish a nearby Nazi supply depot. Pope Pius XII felt the quake caused by the bombardment and rushed to the window of his apartment facing San Lorenzo. He shuddered at the sight of the thick black smoke rising over that quarter of the city and went there at once to comfort his flock. There are poignant photos of Papa Pacelli standing in front of the ancient shrine, surrounded by the frightened men, women and children of the district. With his white soutane soaked with the blood of many of those he had comforted, he wept all the way back to the Vatican.

At war's end, reconstruction on San Lorenzo soon commenced. Today the pilgrims can see it in much the same splendor as did their counterparts eight hundred years ago.

Saint Helena and the Church of Santa Croce

In the quiet, tree-lined Lateran quarter of Rome, six blocks east down the Via Carlo Felice from the Basilica di San Giovanni, stands the ancient church of *Santa Croce in Gerusalemme* (Holy Cross in Jerusalem). Established by the Emperor Constantine at the entreaty of his aged and pious mother, Helena, Santa Croce takes its name from the remarkable relics it houses.

To appreciate the true splendor and significance of this beautiful church one must go back through the ages to that first Good Friday, to a hill just beyond the walls of old Jerusalem, to a spot called "Golgotha," or skull place. Here, as the sun dimmed in the heavens, Jesus was crucified, flanked by two thieves executed in the same fashion. After this momentous event, which altered the course of the world and mankind for all eternity, Jesus was entombed in a sepulchre provided by the kind Joseph of Arimathea. The executioners (Roman occupation troops) dug a ditch at the site in which to bury the instruments they had used—crosses, nails, swords—along with the crown of thorns that had been used to humiliate Jesus. These items were considered defiled by the use made of them.

Following the ascension of our Lord forty days later, it is said that Golgotha became a center of pilgrimage to the small band of disciples living in the area. According to a story that has been handed down, each day they would climb the sloping, cobblestoned Via Dolorosa to pray on the soil sanctified by the blood of their divine Master and over the relics of his suffering. This daily pious trek through the streets of Jerusalem angered the pagan mob. From time to time this anger would erupt into violence against the tiny Christian community. Such incidents continued on into the next century.

Early in his reign the Emperor Hadrian (117–138), annoyed with such a petty provincial problem, decided to obliterate the Christian memorial by raising over the site of Jesus' sepulchre and the ditch on Golgotha two enormous temples—one to Jupiter, the other to Venus.

"Fool!" one Christian historian later wrote. "He thought he could conceal from mankind the glory of the sun which had risen over the world! He failed to see that while aiming to erase the holy places from people's memories, he was rather, quite effectively and vividly, marking their exact position. He could not understand that on the day decreed for the liberation of the Church, the impure columns of his temples would be conspicuous and infallible indicators for the discovery of the sacred sites."

So the emperor, in part, got his wish. The Christians stayed away. But they handed on, from generation to generation, the knowledge that Hadrian's marble edifices rested upon the scene of the redemption of the world. Nearly two centuries later, an incident took place in far-off Rome that was to set off a long chain of events leading to the recovery of the Cross of Christ: Constantine's vision on the Milvian Bridge.

His aged and devout mother soon embraced Christianity and was seized with a fervent desire to recover the True Cross, source of such good fortune for her son and symbol of the salvation of the human race. "I must raise the Cross from the dust!" she declared. Despite her advanced age—she was now in her eighties—and failing health, Helena set sail for Jerusalem. There, full of zeal for the new faith and for her special mission, she walked about at the holy site where, upon her son's orders, Hadrian's pagan temples were being torn down to make way for two Christian churches—the "Marytrion," over the place of the crucifixion, and the "Anastasis," above the sepulchre of our Lord. In the midst of the rubble from all the razing and construction work, Helena probed the ground and prayed for a sign from heaven. One day her prayers were answered. She urged the workmen to begin digging in a certain spot. Before long the laborers came upon a small block of wood. Digging it out, they brushed off the soil to read its inscription, in three different languages: Hebrew, Greek and Latin. It read: *Iesus Nazarenus Rex Iudaeorum*, I.N.R.I.—Jesus of Nazareth, King of the Jews. Their find was electrifying—the inscription Pontius Pilate had ordered affixed to the Cross of the Savior.

The workers continued their efforts, more feverishly than before. In a short time three whole crosses were unearthed, sending more thrills through the group of witnesses. Their rejoicing, however, was tempered by the fact that there was no way to determine which of the three crosses was that of Jesus. The I.N.R.I. block was detached and therefore of no help in identifying it. Standing with Helena was Macarius, the beloved bishop of Jerusalem, who suggested invoking divine intervention. He conceived a test. In a nearby house a woman lay dying. The bishop had all three crosses carried to her bedside. When he touched the first of the crosses to her body nothing happened. The second cross also produced nothing. But upon being touched with the third, the woman at once rose from her bed and walked unassisted through her dwelling, praising the Lord for her miraculous cure. The excellent state of preservation of all three crosses was due to several factors: 1) not all kinds of timber rot with the same speed; 2) hard woods in particular resist decay; 3) the arid and rocky soil of the region would tend to prolong the life of wood imbedded in it.

But perhaps it was Hadrian again who unwittingly did the Christian world a great favor. For the two temples he had ordered built there would certainly have prevented rain from penetrating through to the soil where the crosses were interred, thereby helping to bring about the preservation of the wood. Helena's solemn mission, then, had been accomplished—the crowning achievement of her long life. A few days later she embarked for Rome, bringing with her a portion of the Cross, part of the cross of the good thief, the I.N.R.I. block, and some thorns and nails which the diggers had also unearthed. On board the sailing vessel there was also a cargo of many sacks of soil from the hill on which Christ died.

Arriving in the imperial capital, Helena quickly set about

having a church built into one of the halls of her residence, the Sessorian Palace as it was called. The dirt that she brought back from Jerusalem was spread over the grounds of her property. Hence the new church took its name from the precious relic it possessed and from the soil around its base: *Basilica Sanctae Crucis in Hierusaleme*, the Basilica of the Holy Cross in Jerusalem.

The earliest mention of a house of worship here occurs in the writings of Pope St. Sylvester (314–335): "Constantine dedicated a basilica in the Sessorian Palace where in a gold reliquary are kept pieces of the Holy Cross, and he named this church 'Hierusalem.'" Over the centuries since, the basilica has undergone many restorations and many architectural changes.

Under Pope Gregory II, in the early eighth century, Santa Croce was extensively restored. In the late tenth century, Benedict VII added the adjacent monastery, now inhabited by Cistercian monks. Pope Lucius, in 1144, converted Santa Croce into a three-aisled basilica, with pillars separating the nave from the two side aisles. He also added the campanile, one of the most beautiful Romanesque belltowers to grace the skyline of Rome. In 1492, Cardinal di Mendoze and Pope Alexander VI carried out further alterations. To them goes the credit for the gilded ceiling and the magnificent frescoes by Antoniazzo Romano in the apse, depicting the finding of the True Cross by the saintly empress. Alexander also had constructed the double staircase leading down into the chapel of St. Helena. This small oratory had been originally ornamented with mosaics by Galla Placida, but these were supplanted by a work of Peruzzi in the early 1500s, a masterpiece that shows our Lord together with the four Evangelists, Saints Peter and Paul, St. Helena and Pope Sylvester II, who died while saying mass in Santa Croce. In preparation for the Holy Year of 1750, Benedict XIV engaged the little-known architects Domenico Gregorini and Pietro Passalacqua to give the church its present appearance. Today, rising out of a small piazza is the marvelous facade. The visitor to Santa Croce first passes through a spacious, airy vestibule into a dimly lit interior with three aisles marked by pilasters and eight columns of

Church of Santa Croce

Egyptian granite. The high altar is canopied and has beneath it an antique urn containing the bodies of the martyrs Anastasio and Cesario. The wonderful frescoes of the vault of the tribune are by one of the giants of the Renaissance, Pinturicchio. In the buildings to the rear of the church, remains of a large palace can be traced.

To the left of the sanctuary, a door leads to a hall adorned with the Stations of the Cross. On the wall as you enter is a glass-enclosed slab of wood over which is this inscription: *Crux Boni Latronis,* Cross of the Good Thief. From here a graceful staircase leads up to the goal of all pilgrims, the Chapel of the Relics of the Passion. Over the small altar is the reliquary containing a portion of the cross brought back by Helena, along with the I.N.R.I. inscription, two nails used to fasten Christ to the cross and some thorns from the crown. There is also a fragment of the finger of St. Thomas, thought to be the one with which he probed the wounds of Jesus.

Here is one of the most sacred shrines in all of Christendom. Here, at Santa Croce in Gerusalemme, can be had one of the most precious of spiritual experiences on earth. Standing here in this intensely quiet and awesomely holy place, one trembles with the same emotions that must have swept over St. Helena as she knelt on Golgotha that day so long ago.

The Basilica of Saint Sebastian, Soldier and Martyr

O ut on the Appian Way, about two miles beyond the walls of Rome where it intersects with the Via delle Sette Chiese, rises the Basilica of Saint Sebastian. Beneath the church are catacombs which also bear his name.

This area of the Roman campagna was known in antiquity as *catacumbas*—the hollows—because of a natural depression in the terrain. Ancient documents suggest that it was in a subterranean pagan burial ground on this site where the bodies of the apostles Peter and Paul were interred immediately following their executions. The area eventually gave its name to all such underground cemeteries. Eighteen months later, legends say, the remains were transferred to their final resting places—Peter's to a grave in the Vatican Meadows, Paul's to the location of his beheading along the road to Ostia.

Another story handed down through the ages is that during the violent persecutions of Valerian (253-259), the Christian flock of Rome, in order to prevent their desecration, brought the apostles' bodies back here to be placed in temporary, secret graves. Scholars have yet to agree on where the truth lies, but what is known for certain is that twenty years after Constantine put a stop to the persecutions, Pope Julius and the emperor Constans erected a large romanesque church over the site, naming it the *Basilica Apostolorum*.

From the sixth century on, however, the church has been called the Basilica of Saint Sebastian, and this is the legend behind it. The son of wealthy parents from northern Italy, the brilliant Sebastian served with distinction in the Roman army and was, in time, promoted to the rank of Tribune of the First Pretorian Cohort. Unable to stand by and watch the savagery of Emperor Valerian toward the Christians, however, the compassionate officer sought to ease their sufferings as much as he could. He would bring food and clothing to the imprisoned and find places of refuge for Christians being sought by the authorities. Indeed, he began to embrace their faith himself. He was rumored to have healed a fellow soldier's dying wife by making the Sign of the Cross over her. His piety and fervor persuaded other officers, and even some public officials, to convert.

When all of this came to the attention of Valerian, Sebastian was sentenced to death. Tied to a pine tree on the Palatine Hill, he faced a firing squad of archers. When a woman friend named Irene came to claim his body for burial, she found Sebastian still breathing. Irene took him to her home, where she nursed him back to health. Once back on his feet, the courageous officer made his way to the imperial palace to plead with Valerian to end the slaughter.

Church of Saint Sebastian on the Appian Way

Stunned, then enraged, the tyrant this time ordered Sebastian taken to the Palatine Stadium and beaten to death, his remains to be cast into the *Cloaca Maxima* (main sewer). Around the same time, Sebastian appeared in a dream to the holy woman Lucina and instructed her thus:

> In the sewer next to the arena you will find my body snagged on a rod. Please take it from there to the catacumbas burial ground for interment at the entrance to the crypt near the Apostles' remains.

The martyred Sebastian soon became a favorite saint of the growing Christian population, his burial place a shrine. A native of Milan (at least according to Ambrose, the archbishop of that diocese from 339 to 397), Sebastian was held up as a model son of the church.

In a homily to his people one Sunday, Ambrose exhorted them: *Utamur exempli Sebastiani martyris cuius hodie natalis est. Hic Mediolanensis oriundus erat*; that is, "Let us follow the example of the martyr Sebastian whose feastday is today. He too came from Milan."

Sometime around the year 600, again on Sebastian's feast day (January 20), Pope Gregory the Great delivered a long sermon . . . *in Basilica Sancti Sebastiani die natali eius* . . . which indicates that the ancient church honoring the apostles had by then been renamed for the soldier-martyr. Throughout the period of the Middle Ages St. Sebastian's intercession was frequently sought by the faithful. He was credited with ending the plague that devastated Rome in 680. In the year 826, Pope Eugene II had Sebastian's relics moved to the Vatican and placed beneath the altar in the Chapel of St. Gregory. Throughout the centuries that followed, pilgrims continued to venerate the empty sepulcher in the catacombs on the Appian Way. Finally, in 1216, the Cistercian monks who occupied the adjacent monastery petitioned Pope Honorius III to restore the holy remains to their original resting place. They have reposed there ever since.

Over the centuries, the Basilica of Saint Sebastian has undergone numerous restorations and changes. The current appearance of the church is the result of work carried out under Cardinal Scipio Borghese at the beginning of the seventeenth century. All that is left of the original exterior are the six granite columns of the portico.

Another distinction enjoyed by this church and its catacombs is that they served as favorite places of pilgrimages for many future saints. Jerome, Bridget of Sweden, Catherine of Siena, Charles Borromeo, Philip Neri, Pius V and countless others spent many hours in prayer here. In a tour of the basilica's catacombs, with one of the monks serving as a guide, the visitor will notice numerous ancient wall scratchings invoking the Apostles (perhaps attesting to their temporary interment there). *Petre ed Paule Petite pro Victore* (Peter and Paul, pray for Victor) reads one; *Paule Petre Rogate pro Erote* (Paul and Peter, intercede for Erote) reads another.

To reach the site today, one must leave the city through the *Porta San Sebastiano* (formerly the *Porta Capena*), where the Appian Way begins, and continue on the old highway until the church comes into view on the right.

San Clemente

Christian pilgrims to Rome, hoping to be swept back across a million yesterdays to apostolic times, ought to make their first stop the church of San Clemente. For more so than St. Peter's in all its splendor, and more so than St. Paul's in all its stateliness, this edifice tangibly peels away the centuries.

San Clemente, just a stone's throw from the Colosseum, is actually three churches superimposed one upon the other, with massive stonework and piles of masonry from three distinct Roman epochs. On this site, Christians have gathered for worship across the two millennia of church history. When Peter was serving as bishop of Rome, there dwelled here a pious priest named Clement, who allowed his residence to be used as a titulus, or house-church.

Everything indicates that Clement belonged to the noble Flavian family which gave Rome three emperors—Vespasian, Titus and Domitian. In the year 88, Clement was elected to the Throne of St. Peter, becoming the fourth pope of the infant church that was then struggling to survive the bloodbaths of the persecutions.

Soon after Domitian was elevated to the purple, he brought the full might and fury of imperial Rome crashing down on the city's small Christian community. Even family ties counted for naught as he issued the order to have his cousins Pope Clement and the consul Flavius, a recent convert, executed. After Constantine put an end to the onslaught against Christianity, the faithful filled the ground floor of Clement's home with rubble and mortar to provide a bedrock foundation for the basilica they were soon to raise on that hallowed ground. From early writers, such as St. Jerome, we learn that this basilica was given the name *San Clemente*, in honor of the martyred pope. Throughout the early Middle Ages, Saint Clement's Church remained one of the most prominent of all the city's Christian shrines. Then in 1084 came the infamous Norman sack of Rome. Beautiful historic Saint Clement's fell victim to the devastation wrought by Robert Guiscard who burned all the public buildings from the Lateran to the Capitoline. The rubble from all the destruction raised the ground level of whole districts throughout the city, including San Clemente's neighborhood.

In 1108 Pope Paschal II began construction of a new basilica atop the remains of the fourth century structure. The half-hidden older church was filled in completely and vanished from human sight for seven hundred and fifty years. Since 1667, San Clemente has been in the care of Irish Dominican priests.

It wasn't until 1857 that the amazing stratification of the property was discovered. During restoration efforts under the supervision of an Irish cleric, Father Mullooly, workmen came upon the church beneath. The priest solicited funds from all over the globe to have the lower edifice completely cleared. The excavations revealed an imposing three-aisled church, with its graceful apse and canopied altar still intact. Well preserved too were numerous eighth-, ninth- and tenth-century paintings and mosaics depicting events in the life of Pope St. Clement. Continued digging deeper underground led Father Mullooly into the very rooms of Clement's home, which in imperial times stood at ground level. Further probing brought yet more to light. Just across a slender alley from this house-church was another pink brick residence whose owner had carved out a room for purposes of worship in another popular religion of the age—Mithraism.

In the *mithraeum* one sees a vaulted ceiling, stone benches for the worshipers and a small altar with fine bas-reliefs showing the Persian deity Mithras sacrificing a bull to the sun. Plutarch tells us that the Mithraic mysteries were first brought to Rome by soldiers of Pompey the Great.

Having visited the lower basilica, one can readily see that Pope Paschal was extremely faithful to its architectural plan in his design of the upper church. That plan included a colonnaded courtyard in front. In this area—called the *atrium*—there remained, throughout the sacred rites going on inside, those taking instructions in the faith prior to being baptized, along with those doing penance for various trespasses, and the more curious among non-believers.

The interior of the upper basilica features all the aspects of a typical medieval church, including a mosaic-adorned apse, a marble baldachino over the main altar and a marble-enclosed *Schola Cantorum*, or choir area. There are also two highly ornamental pulpits—one for the reading of the epistle, the other for the gospel. High upon the soaring triumphal archway framing the sanctuary are mosaics of Peter and his third successor.

Even the very pavement of San Clemente is a masterpiece of art, and a perfect example of the *cosmatesque* marble floor, laid out in striking geometric patterns. And so it is then, that in visiting the beautiful Basilica of San Clemente, on the Via San Giovanni in Rome, one can step out of a twentieth-century vehicle and roll back eight centuries by stepping into the church built by Paschal, roll back eight more by descending a staircase into the church mentioned by St. Jerome, and yet four more by picking one's way down another set of stairs into Clement's house-church of apostolic times—and, while down there, stealing a glance into the dark, damp house of worship of a cult that has long since entered oblivion.

Only in eternal Rome is it possible to enjoy an experience so unique.

The Churches of the Forum

For most people the Roman Forum conjures up images of ruins of ancient colonnaded marble temples, perched upon graceful flights of steps, that once paid homage to the various pagan deities. Few think of the old marketplace and political center as a stretch of real estate crowded with medieval Christian churches. Yet it would be fair to characterize it just that way, for there are today a half dozen—at one time there were seven—Catholic houses of worship in, or bordering on, this relatively small rectangular area in the heart of Rome.

In A.D. 638, the still-intact *Curia*, or Senate House, was consecrated by Pope Honorius I as a church honoring Saint Adrian. As the twentieth century dawned, the edifice was deconsecrated and declared a historic landmark. The archeologist Alfonso Bartoli oversaw the removal of all ecclesiastical accretions in an effort to restore the building to the form it knew under the emperor Diocletian.

From the Curia, a hundred-yard stroll down the Via Sacra—the ceremonial road that traverses the length of the Forum—brings us to the thousand-year-old church of *San Lorenzo in Miranda*. Built into the sturdy ruins of the Temple of Antoninous Pius and Faustina, San Lorenzo's evoked Raphael's observation that "today's Rome was built from the wreckage of yesterday's Rome." The epithet "Miranda" (awe-inspiring) probably alludes to the fact that the temple had been one of the most beautiful in all of Rome. A flight of twenty-one marble steps leads up to the porch of the temple and the front door of the church. Not often open, *San Lorenzo's* is approached by an alley leading from the major thoroughfare of Via dei Fori Imperiali.

Almost directly across the Forum from this point, at the end of a narrow path between the Temple of Castor and Pollux and the house of the Vestal Virgins, we come upon the basilica of *Santa Maria Antiqua*. Old Saint Mary's, built at the base of the Palatine

San Lorenzo in Miranda down in the Roman forum

Hill, is the oldest and most important Christian shrine in the Forum, dating to the late fifth century.

Fashioned out of a monumental vestibule erected by Domitian as an entranceway to the imperial palace high overhead on the Palatine, Santa Maria Antiqua has seen numerous restorations. Its interior is noteworthy for several striking seventh-century paintings. Recrossing the Forum to regain the Via Sacra, we turn right past San Lorenzo and presently reach the church of *Saints Cosmas and Damian*, the work of Pope Felix IV in A.D. 527. The pontiff used the circular Temple of Romulus as the vestibule and the rectangular *Templum Atmae Urbis* right in back of it as the church proper. In the *Atmae Urbis*, from the era of Vespasian, were housed the archives of the Censor and other municipal records.

The two Syrian saints honored here were martyred during the savage persecutions of Diocletian. They were physicians who ministered to the poor out of love and without payment. Entombed beneath the main altar, they are venerated as the patron saints of doctors, dentists and pharmacists.

Our stroll on the Via Sacra now continues past the gigantic, gutted, vaulted shell of the Basilica of Maxentius, up a steady incline to the eastern end of the forum. At this juncture visitors of old would behold the majestic and dignified beauty of the Temple of Venus. We, however, now stand before the church of *Santa Francesca Romana*, Saint Frances of Rome.

Originally built in the ninth century by Pope Leo IV and called Santa Maria Nova, the church was given its current name in 1608, after Paul V canonized the late and beloved Frances. Born in Rome in 1384, she wed a wealthy nobleman. Widowed after forty years of a happy and loving marriage, Frances became the first Benedictine lay oblate and devoted her remaining years to caring for the poor and the sick. Beneath the high altar repose the remains of the saint. Also worthy of mention is the tomb of Gregory XI, who in 1377 brought the Papal Court back from Avignon to Rome, from the banks of the Rhone to the banks of the Tiber.

The tall, slender bell tower of the church was added in the twelfth century. Crowned by a cross and soaring high above its surrounding structures, the campanile of Santa Francesca Romana is looked upon as the landmark and guardian of the Christian Forum. A dusty path to the right of the church leads past the Arch of Titus. This first-century monument remains in a perfect state of preservation, in defiance of the tyranny of time.

From this point, the Via San Bonaventura, a narrow leafy lane, begins its ascent to the Palatine Hill. In just a few meters, we come to the tiny medieval church of *San Sebastiano al Palatino*, rising out of a small vineyard and over the site of a shrine erected by

Tiberius to honor his deified predecessor, Augustus. Nearby there once stood also a small but impressive temple to Jupiter Stator. There is an almost sylvan loveliness to this spot, especially in spring when the lane is blossom-strewn and exotic flowers break out in all the crannies of the porous travertine marble of the church.

A little further up the slope is the *Church of San Bonaventura*. In addition to the remains of Bonaventure, cardinal and archbishop of the neighboring diocese of Albano in the late 1200s, the church also contains the body of Blessed Leonardo, who originated the devotional practice of the Stations of the Cross. For that reason, this stretch of the narrow road is flanked by Stations of the Cross.

Thus concludes our pilgrimage to the churches of the Roman Forum. Ah, the Roman Forum! No more evocative term can be found in any language. Once the place to go to hear a fiery oration delivered by a toga-clad statesman, it lives on in our time as a place to go to hear a solemn mass, celebrated by a chasuble-clad priest.

The Churches of
the Aventine

By the reign of Julius Caesar, one hundred years before the Christian era, Rome's Aventine Hill had developed into a dignified district of fashionable private homes, majestic temples and elegant public gardens. Romans were attracted to the area by its rich vegetation and pleasing fragrances, by its soft air and gentle winds. ("Aventine" probably derives from the Latin *ventus*—wind.) The affluent residents of this quarter also delighted in the sweeping vistas afforded by the elevation. From the northern summit, which drops precipitously to the Tiber, they could study the graceful bend of the river and look over into the newly-developing Transtiberim precinct. From the east, they could watch the chariot races down in the Valley Murcia, in the Circus Maximus. Looking beyond and above the Circus, they could thrill to the sight of the sprawling Imperial Palace.

The architectural importance of the Aventine stemmed largely from three strikingly beautiful temples—one to Diana, one to Juno, one to Jupiter. Not far from these were the lavish yet elegant Baths of Decian.

Today the Aventine is still distinguished by its fashionable private villas and its awe-inspiring religious shrines. But whereas pagan temples originally accounted for the grandeur of the neighborhood, Christian churches, since the Edict of Milan, have filled that role.

To reach this picturesque area, start at the Colosseum and head west along Via San Gregorio, and turn right at Via del Circo Massimo. You will soon come upon the bronze statue of Giuseppe Mazzini, the brains behind Italy's *Risorgimento.* This monument is majestically set in the graceful Piazza Romolo e Remo. From this point the sun-dappled Via Terme Deciane begins its climb, twisting and turning until it drops off in the Piazza Santa Prisca. This is as good a spot as any from whence to set out to explore the churches of the Aventine.

The first, the ancient and storied *Santa Prisca*, stands on a natural rise in the terrain, overlooking the square by the same name. It is a modest structure, set back from the street in a narrow courtyard approached by a short flight of well-worn marble steps. The baroque front was the creation of the architect Lambardi in 1600. Behind its modesty of size and appearance, however, lies a long, rich, fascinating history.

In apostolic times this was the home of a pious Jewish couple. When Claudius ordered the expulsion of all Jews from Rome, these two sought asylum in Corinth where, legend has it, they crossed paths with St. Paul and forged a friendship with him:

> After that Paul left Athens and went to Corinth. There he found a Jew named Aquila, a native of Pontus recently arrived from Italy with his wife Priscilla. An edict of Claudius had ordered all Jews to leave Rome. Paul went to visit the pair, whose trade he had in common with them and they worked together as tentmakers. (Acts 18:1–3)

In time, the exiled Jews made their way back to Rome. Aquila and Priscilla returned as converts to Christianity and allowed their home on the Aventine to be used as a place of Christian worship. A line from Paul's letter to the Romans (16:3–5) reads, "Give my greetings to Prisca and Aquila and to the congregation that meets in their house."

Throughout the city at that time there were, as mentioned earlier, as many as twenty-five such *tituli*, or house churches. When the persecutions ended, the Christian community erected spacious church buildings over these *tituli*.

Digging for restoration work in 1933 led to the discovery of the foundations and walls of a first-century dwelling widely believed to be the home of the couple that Paul met in Corinth. The church interior is admirable for its purity and simplicity, for the graceful beauty of its apse, of its ancient columns, of its faded paintings by an unknown fifteenth-century artist.

From here, a five-minute walk toward the Tiber side of the hill will bring you to another fourth-century church, *Santa Sabina*, which also bears the designation of *titulus*. For here too at Sabina's townhouse, in the earliest days of the church, Christians would gather for worship. This noblewoman was converted to the faith by the example and influence of her fervent maid, Serapis. During the persecution by Hadrian, both women paid with their lives for embracing the gospel of Christ.

The wonderful red brick Romanesque church we see on this site today has remained almost totally unaltered since its construction. Built by Peter, a priest from Ilyria, Santa Sabina's is noted for its huge windows with intricate stone carvings into which are set panes of *silenite*, a forerunner of glass. Widely admired also are the original doors of cypress wood with their eighteen sculpted panels, which perhaps inspired Ghiberti for his doors to the baptistry in Florence. One panel represents Moses at the burning bush; another shows the crossing of the Red Sea, and the journey through the Sinai Desert.

The church was embellished by Pope Eugenius II in 824. Four centuries later, Pope Honorius III (1216–1227) gave the church to the holy priest Dominic, and it was here he founded his Dominican Order and established a friary. It was also on this property that Saint Dominic had his memorable meeting with Francis of Assisi.

The visitor to Santa Sabina's will be impressed by the simplicity of the interior, its harmony of proportions, and its delicate beauty, all flooded with light from the thirty-four large windows high up near the open-beamed ceiling. There is a festive joyous air to this church. One sees in Santa Sabina's a perfect example of the ancient basilica plan—the nave terminating in an apse with the side aisles ending bluntly. Excavations carried out in 1919 revealed the walls of a first-century residence, strengthening the claim of tradition that the church was erected upon the remains of Sabina's home.

Reminders of Saint Dominic are everywhere on these grounds.

If one of the Dominican priests or brothers happens to be about, ask him to show you a small hole in the right wall of the church. Through it you will glimpse, set in a lovely garden, an orange tree that is a descendant of the one planted on that precise spot by the saint himself seven hundred years ago. Then ask to be shown the perfectly preserved cell upstairs where Dominic meditated long hours each day. Also, let the friar point out to you the small opening with a crude wooden door through which the holy man would look down into his beautiful church or call to one of his friars.

A couple of hundred yards further along the same street one comes upon yet another church, *Sant Alessio*. A robust, honey-colored structure with a slender bell tower, Sant Alessio's is recessed from the street at the end of a pleasing courtyard. Alessio (*Alexius* in Latin) was the son of a prominent Roman senator. They lived next door to a small church of the fourth century, St. Boniface's. The current church is thus sometimes referred to by a double name, *Sant Alessio e San Bonifacio.*

A pious, contemplative individual, Alessio wanted nothing more than the monastic life. According to legend, in order to avoid a marriage arranged for him, the young man fled his father's house and Rome. After nearly two decades of self-imposed exile, he returned as a beggar to live out his days near the mansion of his parents, unknown to them. The same legend tells that the frail Alessio died under the front stairwell of his boyhood home. Pope Honorius III carried out extensive renovations on the old church. In 1750, the building was again altered sharply by Cardinal Angelo Quirini. It is mostly this that we see today.

At the end of the left aisle can be seen a large part of the wooden staircase under which Alessio is said to have died. As you leave this church, you may wish to stop at the doorkeeper's booth to purchase some postcards featuring excellent photographs of Sant Alessio's. The community of priests who live in the adjoining monastery will appreciate your patronage. Known as the *Somaschi*, these men are of a religious order whose work consists mainly in caring for poor and abandoned youths.

A few paces past Sant Alessio's you will come upon one of the smallest yet most romantic of the Eternal City's squares, the *Piazza dei Cavalieri di Malta*. Designed and monumentalized by Piranesi, it looks like one of his famous engravings come to life, or an outdoor set for an opera. On the left of the miniature piazza is the pink stucco palace of the Egyptian Embassy. To the right is the walled-in Territory of the Knights of Malta and our next Aventine church, *Santa Maria del Prioratu*.

This parcel of land enjoys, by treaty with the government of Italy, complete autonomy and serves as the headquarters of the military order renowned for its worldwide charitable works and with whom quite a few nations maintain diplomatic ties. Peer through the keyhole of the immense iron gate and you will see three countries. First notice that the gardens are in the Knights' territory (an "independent country," if one can stretch the application of the term). Look beyond and spot the rooftops of Rome (Italy) and farther in the distance see the dome of St. Peter's (in the Vatican, country number three). While the church on the property is accessible only by special arrangement, views of it may be enjoyed from the portico of our next church, just across Piranesi's piazza.

Sant Anselmo, a Benedictine church, perches on the western ridge and can be seen from many points throughout the city, as could the temples of the imperial age. The soft, pink brick exterior and campanile are a joy to behold. The cypress-lined approach to the church ends in a charming court. From here, a few stairs lead up and into a clover-carpeted colonnaded atrium, at the far right corner of which stands a bronze effigy of Saint Anselm, Archbishop of Canterbury (1092–1109). Attached to the church is the International Benedictine College. Though the youngest of the Aventine churches, built in the late nineteenth century, Sant Anselmo's is no less interesting and attractive than its ancient neighbors.

The Aventine Hill has two summits. To visit the two remaining churches, one must go back down the Via Santa Prisca, cross over the trolley tracks of the Viale Aventino, and climb the lesser summit to *San Saba*. This medieval brownstone church must have been an even lovelier sight a century or two ago, for writers such as Stendhal describe it as standing alone and isolated among orchards and vineyards. Today it is encroached upon by the plethora of sandstone apartment houses that resulted from the turn-of-the-century building boom in this quarter. Dedicated to Saint Saba, an abbot from Cappadocia who died while on a pilgrimage to Jerusalem in 532, the church presents an architecture which is, for the most part, tenth-century.

This land had once belonged to Silvia, a devout woman of Roman high society, whose son Gregory established a monastery on the nearby Coelian Hill. From her own garden she would daily gather and specially prepare vegetables to be sent over to her ascetic son and his fellow monks for their meager meal. Gregory reigned as pontiff from 590 to 604. The church honors him as Pope St. Gregory the Great, his mother as St. Silvia.

While San Saba's alone amply rewards the pilgrim's trek to "the other Aventine," as the Romans call it, there is yet one more church worthy of a visit—*Santa Balbina*, which honors a second-century virgin martyr. An authentic basilica of the late sixth century, Saint Balbina's enjoys a tranquil setting overlooking the jagged outline of the second-century health spa called the Baths of Caracalla.

The Aventine also offers the pilgrim to Rome an idyllic park with a matchless panorama, glimpses of elegant villas set midst oleanders and pines and orange trees, picturesque streets, pastel orange garden walls bedecked with necklaces of rampant purple wisteria. Here, in the midst of clamorous Rome, is a world apart, an appealing world rendered irenic and beautiful principally by the presence of seven great temples to the Lord.

Santa Costanza: From Mausoleum to Church

Among all the edifices left to us from those days long gone by when Rome served as the capital of a sprawling empire, perhaps the best preserved and least altered is the church of *Santa Costanza*. To reach it, one must leave Rome by the gate named *Porta Pia* and travel about a mile and a half out along the old consular road of the Via Nomentana.

This attractive, red-brick circular structure was not erected as a house of worship but rather as a tomb, in the early years of the fourth century. To appreciate the extraordinary history of this place, however, requires a familiarity with the poignant story of a beautiful thirteen-year-old Roman girl called Agnes. As a devout Christian, during the Emperor Diocletian's persecution, Agnes had taken a vow of perpetual virginity to honor her divine Master. During a round-up of practitioners of the "forbidden cult," Agnes was cast into prison for several days to await her execution. Death came violently to the pious maiden when the prefect of the city commanded one of his deputies to plunge a sword into her throat. Her mortal remains were claimed by her bereaved family for interment on the grounds of their country estate out along the Nomentan Road. The girl's memory was held in the highest esteem by the primitive Christian church and her name has remained synonymous with maidenly purity through the ages since. Saint Agnes was early adopted as the heavenly patroness of young girls throughout the Christian world.

In A.D. 324 Constantine still held the imperial throne. Early that year, his daughter Constantia was stricken with what seemed for certain to be a horrible and fatal illness. Though still a pagan, she clung to a faint hope that if she implored the intercession of the holy virgin Agnes, a miraculous cure might result. Legend

Church of Santa Costanza

informs us that one soft, moonlit evening awash in the sweet fragrance of lilacs, Constantia, wracked with pain, journeyed on foot to pray at the tomb of the young martyr. As she uttered the final words of her prayer, Constantia at once felt a total physical transformation back to her normally excellent state of health.

When she returned to her family in the palace, the news she bore was received with unbounded joy. In celebration the emperor gave orders for the entire city to be decorated in garlands, bunting and banners. At Constantia's request, Constantine arranged for her to be baptized with great pomp and pageantry at the precise spot of her miraculous recovery. Also at her urging, the emperor ordered the construction of a magnificent basilica directly over the tomb of Agnes.

When, some years later, his daughter succumbed to a subsequent illness, Constantine raised a handsome rotunda to house the elaborately carved sarcophagus of red porphyry containing her remains. The grieving father chose, as the site of his daughter's mausoleum, the gardens adjacent to the Basilica of Saint Agnes. Thus it is here, to this day, that among the olive and almond trees rises one of the jewels of early Christian (or late Roman) art.

About sixty-nine feet in diameter, the rotunda has an inner ring of twenty-four pairs of granite columns crowned in the Corinthian order. These are topped with oblong cornices on which rest the supporting arches of the great fenestrated dome. The space between this inner colonnade and the wall features a vaulted ceiling with still-brilliant fourth-century mosaics. These show flowing designs of rich flora and vines laden with bunches of ripe grapes. The mystic and religious sense of this symbolism is made clear by the following passage from the *Acts of St. Eugenia*: "Now is the time of the vintage, when the rich grapes shall be severed from the slender vines to be pressed into the heavenly cups," an allusion, no doubt, to the chalice and wine used in the Christian rituals. The centuries that followed saw the mausoleum put to use as a baptistry for the adjoining basilica. In 1256, Pope Alexander IV converted the circular burial vault into a church. The pontiff directed the clergy of St. Agnes' to transfer the body of Constantia from the sarcophagus to a specially-carved niche within the altar of the newly consecrated "church-in-the-round." It henceforth became known as the Church of Santa Costanza, the Italian rendering of the Latin name.

Five centuries more were to pass before any other changes were made. In 1779 or thereabouts, Pope Paul VI had the precious but empty sarcophagus removed to the Vatican, where it can now be admired in the Pio-Clementine wing of the *Museo Vaticano*. A replica of the sarcophagus stands in its original place.

A stop at Santa Costanza's evokes mixed feelings and pushes back the frontiers of a fervent Christian's emotional limits. Here is hallowed ground indeed. On the one hand, there is an ineffably strange and spectral mood that first engulfs the onlooker. One comes close to hearing, in the mind's ear, the faint echo of a distant funeral dirge and the sobs and moans of the approaching cortege. On the other hand, the heart fairly leaps with a childlike joy at the sun pouring warmly through the upper windows in wide shafts, bathing the entire interior in golden light.

Santa Costanza's, a favorite of Roman brides, is particularly magnificent when decorated for a wedding, with chairs clad in lush green velvet set on either side of the central aisle, which is carpeted in red, and the altar, flanked by dozens of potted palms emerging from an embankment of flowers.

How memorable it is to exit from this unique place into the warm Roman air redolent of moss on old stones and glance back, as the swifts go into their free fall and glide back and forth, to behold a structure virtually unchanged by time, man or the elements across the last seventeen centuries. Emperor Constantine might well have stood precisely there on the day of the unveiling of his tribute to his late daughter, nodding his approval at its simple but beautiful lines.

Out here one might think—if only for a fleeting moment—that Imperial Rome had never passed away.

San Stefano Rotondo

High atop the verdant Coelian Hill in Rome is a narrow walled-in lane that leads to the ancient church of *San Stefano Rotondo*, Saint Steven's-in-the-Round. For the true student of the past, this immense circular Christian house of worship, raised out of the stones of a first-century market, should be a must stop on any sojourn in the Eternal City. Pervasive here is a vague and wistful melancholy mood of abandonment. The throngs of tourists and pilgrims that invade St. Peter's, the Colosseum, Trevi Fountain and all the other well-known attractions, are never to be encountered here. St. Steven's is truly off the beaten trail, in a city with few trails left that have not been thoroughly

San Stefano Rotondo

beaten. As one approaches the entrance, the romantic mystery of ancient Rome clutches at the heart. There is a sense of the centuries peeling away, of a moody yet beautiful bond with the past, the likes of which Goethe, Stendhal and others raved about in their Roman diaries.

Turning off the walled-in lane, the visitor passes through a small, dusty, leafy, picturesque courtyard and comes to an antiquated portico supported by four marble columns. This leads into the vast rotunda built to house and honor the mortal remains of the protomartyr Stephen. Legend says these were moved here from Jerusalem, where in the very first days of the new church, he was stoned to death. Perhaps it was because the name *Stephanos* meant wreath, or circlet, that the Christian community symbolically chose this style of architecture.

Erected some time in the 460s, as the Roman Empire agonized through its death throes, St. Steven's Church used as its nucleus the *tholus*, or central domed structure of the *Macellum Magnum*, the meat market of Nero's Rome. A coin representing this market agrees with the architecture of the church. In his history of Rome, Dio Cassius mentions the place: "Then Nero celebrated a feast and dedicated the market where meat is sold." Pope St. Simplicius (468–482) consecrated the edifice and dedicated it to St. Steven whose cult was widely practiced in Rome at that time. The airy vestibule of the church is paved, interestingly, with fragments of porphyry taken from the *Marmorata*, old Rome's dock used for unloading marbles transported up the Tiber.

San Stefano Rotondo features fifty-eight granite columns forming three concentric aisles supporting a timber roof. The first circle consists of twenty-two Ionic columns, all borrowed from older monuments around the city. The second and larger circle is made up of thirty-six columns with varying capitals. The third ring of original columns was bricked in to form the outer wall we see today. This was done in 1452 under the order of Pope Nicholas V, who feared the ancient structure was in danger of collapsing. In the late 1500s, Pope Gregory XIII had this wall frescoed by Tempesta and Pomarancio, who chose as their theme the martyrdom of the early

Christians and painted graphic scenes of slaughter. Soon after the completion of these paintings, the parents of Rome's children developed a practice of bringing them to San Stefano Rotondo to study the scenes and to have seared on their consciousness and consciences the price their spiritual forebears were willing to pay for the faith. Another Gregory is honored here at St. Steven's. Pope St. Gregory the Great (590–604) was fond of preaching here. Near the entrance is the ancient wooden throne from which that pious and beloved pontiff delivered some of his homilies.

A visit to this holy place is a never-to-be forgotten experience, spiritually and intellectually. One shall forevermore see in the mind's eye, as in the dusky path of a dream, that enormous red brick drum rising out of the pines and cypresses, ilexes and oleanders. Up here, the soft sweet music of silence is a welcome change from the din at the bottom of the hill, where vehicular and pedestrian traffic swirls noisily around the Colosseum.

Even on the sultriest of Roman summer afternoons, the Coelian breezes caress the cheek. The mere sight of the majestic and mysterious church of San Stefano Rotondo, along with the smell of damp marble and moss-covered brick, is enough to distract the mind and beguile the soul.

San Teodoro

The often overlooked yet richly historic circular church of *San Teodoro al Palatino* nestles snugly into the western flank of the Palatine Hill, at the site of the *Lupercal,* the cave where legend says Faustulus came upon the infant twins Romulus and Remus being suckled by a she-wolf.

Erected in the late fifth century, when the mighty Empire was on its deathbed, this rotunda of sun-baked bricks honored a martyr-soldier from the East. Born of a noble family, Theodore had enlisted, when still a youth, in the imperial army in 306. While on a tour of duty at Pontus in Asia Minor, he informed his commander that he would not obey an order to participate in rites to the pagan deities: "I shall never engage in idolatrous worship. Until my last breath I shall confess only Christ." Declining numerous opportunities to recant, Theodore was sentenced to death by fire. His cult soon spread to the West. In the capital, Christians who sought his intercession in heaven built a small oratory in his name, on ground considered sacred by the authorities since it bore witness to the very birth of Rome.

Originally the church served more as a center for the distribution of food and other provisions to the poor. This was perhaps designed to replace the *Annona,* the state food warehouse from which free grain had been doled out to the plebian masses. Legends suggesting this area as the place of the city's origins seem to be supported by sixteenth-century archaeological discoveries and by documents stating that such finds took place *iuxta ecclesiam Sanctum Theodorum.*

In 1845, the antiquarian Vescovali unearthed here foundations of walls thought to be the fortifications raised by Romulus. Also retrieved nearby was the fabled Etruscan she-wolf. Dionysius maintains that the bronze wolf had always been enshrined in a round temple to Romulus that once stood here. In fact, some classical

Church of San Teodoro al Palatino

scholars suspect that the church owes its circular form to having been built into the ruins of such a pagan shrine. Set back from the road, the church of San Teodoro is approached through a time-worn semicircular cobblestone courtyard, in the center of which is a small travertine pagan *ara* bearing the inscription: "On this altar, incense is offered to the gods."

San Teodoro's vestibule adds to the mood of antiquity about the whole place. It is paved with pieces of porphyry found near the *Marmorata*. Within the church proper, there is a delicate sanctuary that culminates in a graceful apse adorned with seventh-century mosaics. Christ is shown flanked by Peter and Paul, along with Theodore and an unknown fellow martyr. While the edifice has undergone numerous restorations—including a major facelift by Pope Nicholas for the Holy Year of 1450—it faithfully retains its ancient Byzantine character.

San Teodoro, affectionately called "San Toto" by the Romans, has long been considered the patron saint of the newborn. Through the ages the faithful have been bringing their sick infants here to be cured through the intervention of "Toto the Wonder Worker."

The church is also known for being the seat of one of the oldest and most esteemed religious societies of Rome, the Arch-confraternity of the Holy Name of Jesus. Members are called the *Sacchoni Bianchi* for the long white robes and hoods they wear during ceremonies. In eras past, their practice was to devote each Friday to wandering the city seeking alms for the destitute. Today the confraternity employs more modern methods of raising funds and collecting goods.

The Church of *Quo Vadis*

This small church owes its origin and name to a story passed down through the centuries about a meeting St. Peter is said to have had with the Lord Jesus. In the second year of the reign of Claudius, the story goes, Peter came to Rome. As we reckon time, that would be sometime in the year A.D. 42. Having walked for several days along the already ancient Appian Way from a port near Naples, the rugged fisherman from Galilee aimed to carry out the Lord's mandate to spread the Good News to all nations from the Eternal City.

As the first bishop of Rome, he set out to serve and to expand the Christian community there. Somewhere about the year 60, the apostle Paul reached the city and, though under house arrest, also began to preach and teach the Christian message to the Roman populace. These two leaders and the church were, for the most part, left unhampered and unharassed in their activities. The view of official Rome was that these *Christiani* were merely a harmless, fanatical sect within the Jewish community.

In the year 64, the government's position and policy suddenly changed. On the nineteenth of July, in the midst of a devastating heat wave and drought, Rome went up in flames. A fire that had taken hold in the wooden grandstands of the Circus Maximus quickly raged out of control, spreading through the tenement-crowded city until eleven of the fourteen precincts established by Caesar Augustus were swept up into the roaring inferno. When the conflagration had spent itself ten days later, Nero looked for a scapegoat to defuse the growing suspicion, among the wretched survivors, of imperial arson. The idea came to Nero to accuse the Christians. The tyrant accused the entire Christian community of arson, subversion and even cannibalism. This last he supported by quoting from Christian writings: "Unless you eat flesh and drink blood you shall not have life in you." Issuing an edict outlawing

Church of *Quo Vadis* on the Appian Way

the faith, he commenced the persecutions and ordered the arrest of local Christian leaders, including the bishop.

Peter now had to go into hiding, lodging with different friends, never staying more than a night or two in one place so as to elude Nero's agents. When the net drew close around him, Peter reluctantly heeded the suggestion of his followers to flee the city. At last they were able to convince him that he would be of greater service to the church alive in exile, than dead in Rome. On a sultry night some weeks after the fire, Peter made his lonely way through the

Capena Gate and down the same great south road by which he had come to Rome, aiming to reach the Adriatic port of Brundisium, where he would set sail to Greece. Weary and saddened, he must have been a study in pathos as he trod the basalt stones of the highway, past the eerie yet romantic silhouettes of cypresses and umbrella pines, through the enormous shadows of the magnificent mausolea of Roman high society. At about the one-mile marker, near the junction of the Via Appia and the Via Ardeatina, the blackness of the night was pierced by a blinding white light. Dazzled, Peter rubbed his tired eyes and peered into the radiance. Engulfed in the light was his divine Master, who had died on Golgotha and ascended to heaven more than three decades earlier. Observing Christ walking toward the gates of Rome, the Apostle asked, trembling: *Quo vadis, Domine?* "Where are you going, Lord?"

To Peter's question Christ replied: *Venio Roman iterum crucifigi*—"I come to Rome to be crucified again." Peter took this as a reproach for his weakness, for abandoning his people and forsaking his mandate. The Lord was willing to suffer the agonies of the Cross all over again if that is what it would take to save the church in Rome. Peter wept ashamedly, apologized profusely, bid farewell to his Master and returned to the city on the Tiber to resume his apostolic mission. In time, the authorities tracked him down. He and Paul were cast into the Mamertine Prison and its dreaded Tullianum Dungeon. For nine months they were subjected to starvation and scourgings, and to the most unspeakable atrocities, until the day that an order was handed down sentencing them to death. The bishop of Rome was crucified in Nero's arena on Vatican Hill. The Apostle of the Gentiles was beheaded about a mile beyond the walls, on the road to Ostia. Over the first site, two and a half centuries later under Constantine, rose the great Basilica of St. Peter. At the same time the Basilica of St. Paul's Outside the Walls was built at the site of Paul's execution.

The story of Peter's encounter with Christ continued to be passed along from generation to generation, down through the ages. In the ninth century, devout Christians marked the spot with a little church named for the question Peter addressed to Jesus: *La*

Chiesa di Quo Vadis? the Church of "Where Are you Going?" In its thousand-year history, the chapel has undergone many restorations and embellishments. Its present appearance, including the soft pink outer walls, dates to 1637.

Just inside the door is a block of paving stone with the impression of a pair of feet. A legend maintains that these are the footprints of Christ, seared into the road from the intense heat of the apparition. Scholars submit that the stone is more likely a pagan offering of thanksgiving after a safe journey. On the right wall is a marble plaque explaining in Italian the story of Christ's appearance at this crossroads. To the left of the altar is a painting of Peter's crucifixion. It shows the Apostle hanging on the cross, head down and emaciated. Tradition tells us that Peter's last request to his executioners was that he be crucified thus, since he was unworthy even to die in the same manner as the Lord.

Before leaving the chapel, a visitor should pause to view, near the holy water font, the bust of Henryk Sienkiewicz (1846-1916), author of the historical novel *Quo Vadis.* In it, Sienkiewicz tells the story of the turbulent early years of Christianity in Rome. Polish expatriates living in Italy erected this monument in honor of their Nobel Prize-winning countryman on May 15, 1977.

It has been said that every legend has its foundation in truth, and perhaps that is so. At any rate, each time I leave the Church of Where Are You Going, step back out into the sunlit street and turn toward the walls of mighty Rome, I pause to reflect awhile. For as I pass this way, I might be walking in the very footsteps of the Fisherman *and* the Prince of Peace.

Saint John
Before the Latin Gate

*S*t. *John Before the Latin Gate* is the lyrical name of one of Rome's ancient churches. It might well be also the title of a short chapter in the long history of the Roman Empire. There is an ancient tradition that has come down to us about the naming of this church.

Sometime around the year A.D. 90, a provincial governor felt the need to bring a local problem to the attention of the emperor himself: "To the most pious Caesar, always Augustus, Domitian, the Pro-consul of the Ephesians sends greetings. We wish to notify your majesty that a certain man named John—of the nation of the Hebrews—coming into Asia and preaching Jesus crucified, has affirmed him to be the true God." When the provincial authorities could not deter "John" from his mission by entreaties or threats, the pro-consul sought the emperor's guidance: "Since we have not been able to induce him by any methods to deny his Christ and honor the immortal gods, we humbly ask what your royal pleasure would have us do with him." Tradition holds that the accused was none other than John the Evangelist.

Domitian, brother of Titus and youngest son of the emperor Vespasian, had ruled competently and wisely in the first ten years of his reign (81-90). After a failed revolt of one of his generals, however, he became suspicious, indeed paranoid, about the possibility of other such plots. He became overbearing, infringing on the rights of the Senate, suppressing writers and intellectuals, executing political foes, and persecuting Jews and Christians alike. It was in this mental state that he received the pro-consul's letter.

Growing more livid as he read the message, Domitian exploded in rage and ordered his subordinate to put the holy man in chains and personally escort him from Ephesus to Rome for "proper sentencing." Some weeks later, informed that the prisoner and escort were approaching the city, Domitian and his court, the story goes, went out to the Latin Gate to await them. The emperor then and there ordered the evangelist to be first scourged and afterwards thrown into a boiling cauldron. Not caring to wait around for the sentence to be carried out, Domitian returned to the palace, only to learn later that somehow the condemned man had come forth from the cauldron unharmed. Shaken by the report, the emperor then ordered the disciple of Christ to be banished to the island of Patmos. It was there, tradition maintains, that John had his visions and wrote the Apocalypse.

In the early fifth century, the Christians of Rome commemorated this episode with the building of a charming church, to which they gave the name of St. John's Before the Latin Gate. Tucked away in a tranquil little back alley just inside the circuit of the Aurelian Walls, the small brown brick edifice features a beautiful arcaded entrance and a graceful belltower. The interior is divided into three naves marked by columns of granite and porphyry with Ionic capitals. These came from various pagan buildings, two of them from the abandoned Temple of Ceres and Proserpina.

Sixteen centuries of Christian worshippers have picked their way up the sloping cobblestone lane that leads to the church of *San Giovanni alla Porta Latina*, as the current citizens of Rome know it. Because of its appealing architecture and picturesque setting, the church is favored by young couples for their weddings. Nearby, on the Via Latina, can be seen a small octagonal chapel by the name of *San Giovanni in Oleo*, built in 1509 and said to mark the precise spot of the attempt to boil the evangelist in oil.

Santa Maria degli Angeli

At the height of the most savage of Imperial Rome's persecutions of the Christians, the Emperor Diocletian decided to erect the stupendous bathing complex named for him. Using tens of thousands of Christians as slave labor, he raised a series of spacious halls to house warm rooms, hot rooms, and a swimming pool spanning 2400 square meters.

Taking up the rest of the 130,000 square meters set aside at the base of the Viminal Hill were libraries, gymnasia, conference rooms and gardens. All of this was enclosed by a rectangular wall with round towers at each of the four corners, three of which still exist. Today, the remains of the Baths of Diocletian afford us some idea of the mammoth buildings that sprung up in the declining days of the empire, in the days when Rome gave herself up to the

Santa Maria degli Angeli

luxuries of indolence in spite of the gathering clouds. They make a lasting impression of the physical grandeur of ancient Rome.

In 1091, Pope Urban offered these ruins to St. Bruno for the establishment of a Carthusian monastery, but Bruno and his fellow monks thought the place unsuitable. Five centuries later a humble Sicilian priest, Jacopo del Duca, exhorted Pius VI to do something special with these magnificent ruins to commemorate the Christian martyrs who toiled in the construction of the baths.

Devoted in particular to the Holy Angels, del Duca suggested that a church in their honor be built there. A project so revolutionary as this, Pius thought, could be realized only through the creative genius of Michelangelo. For the last thirty years of his life, this Titan of the Renaissance was practically the official city architect of Rome and was consulted on all construction, renovation and restoration of important buildings. Indeed, he had already been responsible for overseeing all work on the spiritual center of the city (St. Peter's), as well as on the secular center (the Capitoline).

The legendary eighty-eight-year-old Florentine, after studying the floor plan of Diocletian's complex, settled on doing something with the *tepidarium* (the warm room). He drew up plans to convert the great domed hall into a church to be named *Santa Maria degli Angeli*. Michelangelo's design called for a church in the form of a Greek cross—336 feet long, 308 wide. The great nave was to be 74 feet wide and 84 feet high. To commemorate the laying of the first stone in 1563, a papal coin was minted engraved thus: *Cio che prima servi all'uso pagano è ora tempio della Vergine. Fondatore è Pio. Fuggite Demoni!* (That which originally served a pagan function is now a temple to the Virgin. Its founder is Pius. Begone Satan!)

This was to be Michelangelo's final architectural creation. On a sleety February afternoon in 1564, just a few months shy of his ninetieth birthday, he succumbed to a fever and the inexorable toll of old age. The church within the baths, St. Mary of the Angels, was opened and dedicated two years later. Diocletian's *tepidarium* was at last adapted to its new sacred office. The church soon proved to be among the most renowned of Rome's houses of worship.

Pope Clement XI, in 1701, added an unusual touch to things. He asked the help of Francesco Bianchini, the famous mathematician and astronomer, in fixing the date of the celebration of Easter, which sometimes had been erroneously calculated. To dramatize this, Bianchini traced a meridian line in the right transept of the church, latitude 15 degrees, indicated in inlaid marble. On every fair day since, precisely at noon, the sun—coming through an opening in the right side of the transept wall—has cast a shaft of light precisely on this spot.

Under Benedict XIV, in 1749, Vanvitelli made some alterations to Michelangelo's work. He quickly reversed these, however, when a great public cry went up over his presumptuousness in second-guessing the master.

Entrance today is gained through a nondescript opening in the craggy walls that face the Piazza della Republica. One passes through a circular vestibule that features a statue of Saint Bruno, founder of the Carthusian Order. So lifelike is this carving by the great Frenchman Jean Antoine Houdan that Clement XIV used to say of it: "This statue would speak, if speaking were not forbidden" (Carthusian monks customarily keep strict silence).

One step beyond the vestibule there comes into view the splendor of Michelangelo's touch—his high altar punctuating a scene of great space and light. The lofty walls are bedecked by paintings that once graced St. Peter's Basilica. (They were replaced there by more enduring replicas in mosaic.) There's Domenichino's *Martyrdom of St. Sebastian* and Maratta's *Baptism of Jesus.* There's Perugino's *Glory of the Angels* and Batoni's *Fall of Simon Magus*, among others. In the apse, Pius IV reposes in a tomb designed by Michelangelo. To the left of the apse, in a small chapel, lie the remains of the martyrs Prosper, Felix, Aurelia and Eulalia. After his controversial work on the church, Vanvitelli fashioned a cloister and monastery where a community of Carthusians lived in strict silence and seclusion until 1884. Upon their departure, their quarters were transformed into a branch of the National Museum, now known as the *Museo delle Terme.* This continues to provide an ideal setting for an extensive collection of Roman antiquities; countless tombstones and sarcophagi, with enough Latin to keep even the most ambitious translator busy for a lifetime; sculptures, mosaics, urns, and a variety of other excavation finds.

In his worst nightmare, Diocletian, who massacred Christians, could never have envisioned all this taking place in his proud baths. Where sixteen centuries ago gouty Romans worked out their kinks, today Christians genuflect to their God. And today, the only water to be found in the *Thermae Diocletianae* is holy water in small marble basins, at the entrance to the *Ecclesia Sanctae Mariae et Sanctorum Angelorum.*

A Profusion of Churches

So great is the number of churches in Rome that guides, guidebooks, scholars, clerics and the Vatican itself cannot agree on just how many there are. Some sources will say 300, some 400, a few 500. But it all depends on what counts as a church and on what the boundaries of Rome are. Should every little oratory and chapel be included in the count? Should recently-constructed churches in Rome's new suburbs that have proliferated since the last Holy Year be considered? Whatever the verdict, however high or low the final count, it will not affect Rome's reputation as truly *Urbs Ecclesiarum*, the City of Churches.

In addition to those treated at considerable length in these pages, there remain untold dozens of others that merit the attention of the pilgrim with sufficient time (and energy). Here is a catalog of my favorites among all the churches.

SANT ANDREA DELLA VALLE

Opera lovers have a special interest in the church of St. Andrew in the Valley, for it is the setting of the first act of Puccini's *Tosca*. It also has the third largest cupola in Rome. Construction began in 1590. The lavish baroque entrance of travertine was added in 1665 by the architect Rainaldi. St. Andrew's is exceedingly rich in works of art. There are frescoes by Domenichino portraying high-lights in the life of the saint. Mattia Preti did the frescoes of St. Andrew's martyrdom. The tombs of two Renaissance popes are also to be found here: Pius II and Pius III.

SANT ANDREA AL QUIRINALE

From the valley we climb one of Rome's seven hills to find Andrew honored with another church. This Saint Andrew's is also richly adorned and is known as *The Jewel of the Baroque*. One of the great Borromini's finest architectural achievements, it has an elegant Corinthian design. Commissioned by Cardinal Camillo Pamphili, nephew of Pope Innocent X, St. Andrew's on the Quirininal Hill was given to the Jesuits for use by its novices. Among its art works is a magnificent statue of *St. Andrew in Glory*, sculpted by Raggi from a design by Bernini.

SAN BENEDETTO IN PISCINULA

This church is just over the river from the Tiber Island. The name, which translates as "St. Benedict's in the Swimming Pool," derives from the fact that the *frigidarium* of an ancient Roman bath once occupied this site. Benedict himself is said to have lodged in a house nearby at the end of the fifth century, before he left Rome to seek a life of monastic solitude and asceticism at Subiaco. St. Benedict's charming small brown bell tower houses the city's oldest church bell (A.D. 1069). Here the faithful still come to venerate the same painting of the Blessed Virgin before which Benedict is said to have prayed.

SAN CARLO AL CORSO

This church stands above the remains of a very ancient church that bore the name of *San Nicolo del Tufo*. In 1612 the foundation of the present edifice was laid. A half century later the construction was completed with a massive dome by Pietro da Cortona. The church honors St. Charles Borromeo, whose heart is kept behind the high altar in an impressive reliquary. The interior, in the shape of a Latin cross, consists of three naves. Frescoes on the ceiling of the center aisle depict the *Fall of the Rebellious Angels*. Charles Borromeo (1538–1584) became the cardinal archbishop of Milan at the tender age of twenty-three. He is honored with a colossus, the size of the Statue of Liberty, on a cliff over Lake Maggiore where the Borromeo family summered.

CHIESA NUOVA *(New Church)*

This church is more properly called Santa Maria in Vallicella. Documents show that a church to St. Gregory occupied this property back in the twelfth century. In 1575 Pope Gregory XIII requested a church to be built here honoring the Blessed Mother. Leo XI consecrated the new St. Mary's in 1605. Paintings above and flanking the tabernacle were carried out by the Flemish master Rubens in his early career. This church is of special interest to admirers of Pope Pius XII, for he grew up as Eugenio Pacelli in this parish, served here as an altar boy, and was assigned here as a curate soon after his ordination to the priesthood.

SANT EUSTACHIO

Ninth century documents attest to the existence of this church, which commemorates Eustace who rose from private to general in the Roman army, and then suffered martyrdom under Hadrian for refusing to honor the pagan idols. Set in a small irregular piazza by the same name, the church features a beautiful brick campanile of the twelfth century. Under the high altar repose the relics of Saint Eustace, his wife Saint Theophista, and sons Saints Agapetus and Theopestus. All were martyred in the Colosseum by being roasted alive.

SAN FRANCESCO A RIPA

St. Francis' on the Banks was built in the mid-1200s. It is adjacent to a house where Francis of Assisi resided briefly during his visit to Rome to seek the pope's permission to establish a mendicant order. Its ochre front entrance looks out over a public square just a few yards from the edge of the Tiber, on the Trastevere side. The attractive interior is highlighted by a main altar beautifully decorated with columns and colored marbles. There are four side chapels, all richly ornamented. In the chapel to the left of the altar can be seen the exquisite carving of Blessed Ludovica Albertoni, by Bernini.

LA CHIESA DEL GESÙ

The Church of Jesus was built by the Jesuits in the late 1500s. The imposing facade represents strikingly the transition between the Renaissance and Baroque periods. Its spacious interior was purposefully designed to provide a suitable auditorium for preaching, for which the Jesuits were especially renowned. One's eyes are drawn upward into the vast dome with which Giacomo della Porta crowned this great house of worship. In the left transept is the famous altar of St. Ignatius, featuring a fine silver statue of the founder of the order. Visitors may be especially interested in the gold-bronze sarcophagus below the altar, in which reposes the body of Ignatius.

Church of the Gesù

SAN GREGORIO MAGNO

Across the valley from the Palatine stands, perched on the Coelian Hill, the age-old church of St. Gregory the Great. Known for its simple beauty and noble flight of steps, the church occupies the same property where Gregory had his home. Legend tells us that Gregory once served as city prefect but exchanged his political career for the monastic life. In 575 he turned his residence into a Benedictine monastery, taking vows as a monk himself. A story says that the holy man suffered from a delicate stomach and that his mother Silvia (a saint herself) would daily send over a pot of specially-prepared vegetables from her house on the nearby Aventine. Upon the death of Pope Pelagius II in 590, Gregory was summoned by popular demand from the quiet of his monastery to the Chair of Peter. As pope, he was an influential writer. His *Pastoral Care* defined the episcopal ministry as one of shepherding souls. His vigorous promotion of liturgical music gave it the name Gregorian Chant. In the right aisle of the church is a charming little chapel of St. Gregory, and opening off of it is a room said to incorporate in its fabric whatever remains of Gregory's cell.

SANT IGNAZIO

This church was built in 1626 by the Jesuit Order to honor the canonization of Ignatius. The church features one of the most impressive baroque exteriors in Rome. The edifice reminds the visitor of the other great Jesuit church, *Il Gesu*. Frescoes on the ceiling of the center nave, by Andrea Pozzo, give a glimpse of paradise: Christ sending the light of the true faith to St. Ignatius, who in turn brings it to all four corners of the earth. St. Aloysius and St. John Berchmans lie buried under the richly-decorated side altars.

SANT ONOFRIO

Built in 1419, this edifice has been restored many times. The driving force behind its construction on the western flank of the

Janiculum Hill was Blessed Niccolo da Forca Palena, of the Hermits of St. Jerome. Approached by a fine portico of nine archways, the church consists of a single wide nave with two chapels on either side. In 1595 the tormented poet Tasso came to Rome at the bidding of Pope Clement VIII who wished to award him the literary prize of the Crown of Petrarch. Shortly after his arrival, however, Tasso took seriously ill and was housed at Saint Onofrio's where he died. The cell he occupied can still be seen. The adjacent cloister is one of the most beautiful in all of Europe.

LA MADDALENA

The quaint little rococo church to Saint Mary Magdalene occupies its own miniature piazza one short block from the Pantheon. Built in the late seventeenth century, the Maddalena is adorned with superb frescoes of Christ preaching and the raising of Lazarus. The altar is flanked by two sculptures of Magdalene—one representing Mary arriving at the empty tomb, the other showing her encounter with the risen Lord in the garden.

SAN PIETRO IN MONTORIO

"St. Peter on the Gold Mountain" perches on a ridge of the Janiculum Hill. From its steps can be seen sweeping, breathtaking views of Rome and the windings of the Tiber. Founded in the ninth century, it was rebuilt in the fifteenth century by Ferdinand and Isabella of Spain. The church is said by some to occupy the site of St. Peter's crucifixion, but scholars suggest that Peter suffered martyrdom in Nero's Circus in the Vatican meadows. In the courtyard of the adjacent Franciscan convent is the *Tempietto* (Little Temple) by Bramante, a lovely circular domed chapel with sixteen Doric columns. This beautiful adaptation of antique architectural themes was completed in 1498.

SAN SILVESTRO IN CAPITE

This was an important center of pilgrimage because of its reliquary containing part of the head of John the Baptist, hence the name *in capite*. First erected by Pope Stefano III around the year 753, the church has been restored and altered numerous times. The remains of Pope St. Sylvester I repose here. The interior is airy and ornamental, with six side chapels. Recent excavations have revealed that the church stands over the ruins of the colossal Sun Temple erected by the Emperor Aurelian. San Silvestro serves as the national church of the English Catholic community of Rome.

SANTA TRINITA DEI MONTI

A twin-spired church of the late 1400s, it crowns the world's most famous and magnificent staircase, the Spanish Steps. Its hilltop

Church of Santa Trinita Dei Monti atop the Spanish Steps

position and the upward thrust of its two belfries, along with the obelisk in front, make Trinita dei Monti one of Rome's most renowned and beloved landmarks. Charles VII of France built this picturesque shrine to the Blessed Trinity. Its stained glass windows came from Narbonne. Louis XII and subsequent French monarchs further embellished the edifice. The church occupies part of the estate of the second-century general, Lucullus, known for his lavish dinner parties.

SAN VINCENZO ED ANASTASIO

This is a most pleasant little church opposite the Fountain of Trevi. Tenth-century documents mention it under the name of Saint Anastasius. Saint Vincent's name seems to have been added five or six centuries later. The single nave has three chapels on each side. Above the main altar is a fresco of the two patron saints. Especially interesting is the fact that the hearts of twenty popes—from Sixtus V (1585-1590) to Pius VIII (1829-1830)—are encased in reliquaries in the church crypt.

SAN GIORGIO IN VELABRO

Behind the ancient Arch of Janus, just off Piazza Bocca della Verita, stands the church to George the "Great Martyr," one of the most beloved saints among Greek people everywhere. As a soldier serving in Cappadocia, Saint George was executed in the persecution of Diocletian. His skull is believed to be preserved in a reliquary beneath the main altar.

Three wall inscriptions in Greek seem to suggest that the church belonged to a colony of Byzantine Greeks in ninth- and tenth-century Rome. Like the nearby church of Santa Maria in Cosmedin, San Giorgio's has columns taken from various structures of ancient Rome. The high altar has a marble baldachino of the eighth century. A few scattered fragments of medieval frescoes still grace the upper walls.

Church of San Giorgio in Velabro—seen through the arch of Janus

Church of San Giorgio in Velabro

SANT AGNESE IN AGONE

Honored by a church in her name out on Via Nomentana, Agnes, the tender young martyr of Diocletian's reign of terror against the Christians, has another dedicated to her in Piazza Navona. This edifice, according to pious legend, rises over the spot where Agnes suffered her agony and death. What is known for certain is that in antiquity the Stadium of Domitian stood here and that it served as the site of public Christian executions.

The original modest oratory that was erected here in Agnes' honor, soon after the Edict of Milan, was replaced by a more spacious church at the direction of Pope Callixtus II (1123). In 1642 that was razed and the present domed church was built by Innocent X in the mid-seventeenth century. The baroque front is the work of Borromini. Rich in marbles, sculptures, bronzes, and antique columns, the interior is in the form of a Greek cross.

SANT AGATA DEI GOTI

This church dates from the fifth century. It has undergone so many restorations and renovations across the ages that the only remains of antiquity still visible are the twelve granite columns and the mosaic pavement. When the Goths, who were Arians, occupied Rome in 549, they made Saint Agata's their national church, hence the name *dei Goti*. St. Gregory the Great, after purifying the church of the stain of Arianism, reconsecrated it and enshrined some relics of Agata in the main altar.

SANTI APOSTOLI

One of the largest religious edifices in Rome, the original Church of the Holy Apostles was begun by Pope Pelagius I in 556 and completed by his successor, John III. Badly damaged by an earthquake in 1348, the structure was restored by Martin V in 1420. Most of the present church building dates only from the late 1600s. The vastness and ornateness of the interior are impressive.

During renovations in 1873, bodies believed to be those of the apostles Philip and James were discovered in a marble sarcophagus in the crypt beneath the high altar. During his time in Rome, Michelangelo used the Holy Apostles as his parish church. After his death in February of 1564, the artist's body was temporarily entombed here before being taken for permanent burial in the church of Santa Croce in Florence.

SAN NICOLA IN CARCERE

Numerous legends have come down to us about this church, Saint Nicholas in Prison. It stands near the banks of the Tiber in an area which was called in ancient times the *Forum Holitorium*, or vegetable market. One story has it that the church was constructed out of the ruins of the Temple of Piety. Dating to around 165 B.C., this temple was thought to have been commissioned by the Roman Senate to commemorate the filial devotion of a young woman who gave her own milk to her incarcerated mother who had been sentenced to die of starvation.

Another tale claims that the church was fashioned from the materials of three small temples said to have stood here in honor of the gods Janus, Juno and Spes. What is certain is that the church goes back at least as far as the fifth century and honors St. Nicholas of Myra, who died in 342. In a splendid urn of dark green porphyry beneath the altar are said to repose the relics of the martyrs Marcellinius, Faustinius, Simplicius and Beatrice. In the basement can be seen extensive remains of the ancient structure, or structures, on which the church stands. In the campanile are two bells from the thirteenth century.

SANT ANGELO IN PESCHERIA

As the name suggests, this church of the Holy Angel (St. Michael the Archangel) stands in what was once the city's fish market. Its exterior is formed from a colonnade built in 147 B.C. and restored in 23 B.C. by Augustus, who then named it the *Porticus*

Octavia for his sister. It is a classic example of how so much of Christian Rome rose out of the wreckage of pagan Rome. Pope Boniface II (530–532) is credited with the original construction of Sant Angelo in Pescheria, which over the centuries has undergone numerous alterations. In the course of some seventeenth century work on the church a sarcophagus was found beneath the sanctuary. A leaden plaque on the sarcophagus states that the relics of St. Symphorosa and her seven children lie within—all said to have suffered martyrdom in the persecution of Hadrian in A.D. 130.

SAN LORENZO IN PANISPERNA

Believed to have existed as early as the sixth century, this church stands on the supposed site of Saint Laurence's terrible martyrdom. Above the altar is a fresco depicting the deacon's suffering. It is the work of Pasquale Cati, a pupil of Michelangelo.

Several theories are offered concerning the curious phrase "in Panisperna." One suggests that it is for two families, Panis and Perna, who resided in this street in ancient times. Another explanation is that a deaconry existed here where bread *(panis)* and ham *(perna)* were distributed to the homeless.

At one time, the church was in the care of the Order of the Poor Clares. Saint Bridget, the patroness of Sweden, loved to assist in their work and often begged alms on the steps of the church. One story says that the Christ on the crucifix in the sanctuary once spoke to her during one of her long meditations at the altar rail. The church is now in the charge of the Franciscans.

SAN PAOLO ALLE TRE FONTANE

A visit to this unique shrine requires a mini-pilgrimage in itself, for it is located several miles beyond the walls of Rome on the Via Laurentina, at a spot called *Acquae Salviae.* Tradition informs us that a small church was raised here in the fifth century to mark the place of the apostle Paul's decapitation. The *Apocryphal Acts of the*

Apostles relate that Paul was martyred at *Aquas Salvias,* near a pine tree. St. Jerome and other early writers maintain that because of his status as a Roman citizen, he was not crucified but afforded the less ignominious death of beheading.

From certain words of Saint Clement of Rome, who may possibly have witnessed the event, it is thought that the Emperor Nero presided. A small cell under the nearby church of *Scala Coeli* is reputed to have been occupied by the apostle for some hours pending Nero's arrival. One pious legend states that Paul's head bounced three times on the ground, and at each point a spring suddenly flowed, hence the name *Tre Fontane.*

Also on this property is *Santi Vincenzo e Anastasio alle Tre Fontane*, the abbey church of the Trappist monastery here.

SAN STANISLAO DEI POLACCHI

This is the Polish National Church in Rome, located just off the Piazza Venezia on the *Via delle Botteghe Oscure* or "Street of the Dark Shops," so called for a row of dimly lit artisans' shops that stood here as late as the onset of the Renaissance. The street is often host to Polish pilgrimage groups paying a visit to the church named for Stanislaus, patron saint of their homeland. Stanislaus served as bishop of Cracow from 1072 until his martyrdom in 1079 at the hands of King Boleslaus II. Originally an eleventh-century structure in honor of San Salvatore, the church was reconstructed during the pontificate of Honorius IV in 1285. It underwent further alteration in 1580 under Pope Gregory XIII, who then entrusted it to the Polish cardinal Stanislaus Hos for use by his countrymen as their center of worship in Rome, with the adjoining building serving as a hospice for them.

Behind the baroque facade is an impressive interior with a single nave, four small altars along each side wall, and a vaulted ceiling adorned with frescoes depicting the "Glory of Saint Stanislaus." Over the main altar is a sculpture group representing Jesus with Saints Stanislaus and Hyacinth.

SAN LORENZO IN DAMASO

This is a most historic church, believed to have been founded in the residence of the fourth-century Pope Damasus who was famous for, among other things, transforming the tombs of martyrs in the catacombs into beautiful shrines. Columns and other materials from the Theater of Pompey which once stood nearby may have been used in the construction of the original church. In 1494, the church was altered and enlarged by Bramante and incorporated into the *Palazzo Cancelleria*, the papal chancery office building by the same architect. The interior is almost a square with an apse, and it is bounded by arcades on three sides. The body of Pope Saint Damasus reposes under the main altar.

SAN SISTO VECCHIO

"Old St. Sixtus'" church is indeed old, dating to Constantinian times. In its earliest years it was called *Titulus Trigridae*, possibly after the Roman matron who once owned the property. In time, the church was dedicated to and named for Pope St. Sixtus II, who was martyred in the nearby catacombs of St. Callixtus during the persecutions of Valerian. According to an ancient story, the church stands on the site where young Deacon Laurence caught up with the pontiff, who was being dragged to his execution, and begged to be allowed to suffer martyrdom with him. Three days after the death of his beloved pope, St. Laurence met the martyr's end for which he longed.

The church was reconstructed by Pope Innocent III (1198–1216). The outside walls, part of the apse, and the bell tower date from that period. Little remains of the primitive structure. In 1219, Pope Honorius III entrusted the care of the church to the newly-formed Dominican order. St. Dominic himself lived here for a time before taking up residence at Santa Sabina's on the Aventine Hill.

❖

These are but some of the great churches of Rome, a city that one Roman friend of mine characterizes as "a sea of cupolas, an ocean of campaniles." Each church will more than amply reward the pilgrim who takes the time to visit. Each one is a delight to the eye, with its architecture, to the soul, with its art, and to the intellect, with its long and interesting history.

The Marian Churches of Rome

After Rome adopted Christianity, the veneration of the Blessed Mother quickly manifested itself in a profusion of Marian churches throughout the city. No longer was Venus invoked as the protectress of the ancient capital, but rather Mary. Her divine motherhood continues to be celebrated here through the shrines named for her. In the See of Peter there can be no doubt that Mary is indeed the mother of Mother Church herself. Of the Eternal City's more than fifty churches honoring the Virgin Mary, here are some of the most renowned (in addition to Santa Maria Maggiore and Santa Maria in Trastevere).

SANTA MARIA IN ARA COELI

Toward the end of his life the Emperor Augustus (27 B.C.-A.D. 14) wished to see the future, to know who would govern the sprawling empire in his place. One day he climbed to the summit of the Capitoline Hill to consult a sybil who dwelt there. She prophesied that a Hebrew child, recently sent from heaven and born of a virgin in Judea, would one day reign over the whole world. Taking the prophetess at her word, Augustus then erected an altar on the Capitoline with this inscription: *Haec est ara primogeniti Dei* (This is an altar to God's first born Son).

In the late 500s a group of Greek monks built a church there. Dedicated by Pope St. Gregory the Great, the church was named *Santa Maria in Ara Coeli*, Saint Mary's over the Altar of Heaven. In the thirteenth century it passed into the charge of the Franciscans who have been there ever since. Constructed in the romanesque style, the church never did get the marble exterior intended for it. Thus today we see it exactly as did our Christian forebears a millennium and a half ago. Perched high upon the Capitoline, with sweeping views of the Eternal City, Santa Maria in Ara Coeli was for centuries approached by a steep, tree-dotted slope. In 1348, during the Avignon period of the papacy, the one hundred and twenty-four marble steps leading up to the Temple of the Sun on the Quirinale Hill were transferred here. The project was paid for by funds from the Roman people themselves, in gratitude to Mary for the city's survival of the plague at that time.

In our time, the church is as well known for its towering flight of stairs as for its architecture and history. Since the fifteenth century it has been renowned as the repository of the most famous statue of the baby Jesus. The *Bambino Gesu* was carved by a Franciscan from the trunk of an olive tree in the Garden of Gethsemane. This much-venerated image of our Lord as a child was frequently taken to the homes of ailing children and credited with thousands of miraculous cures, until the winter of 1994 when someone broke into the church and stole it. The carving one sees today in a side chapel is a replica.

SANTA MARIA SOPRA MINERVA

As the name "Saint Mary's Over Minerva" implies, this Marian shrine was built upon the ruins of a temple honoring the pagan goddess of war. In gratitude for his military successes in Asia, General Pompey raised this Temple of Minerva in the Campus Martius district. Under the Emperor Domitian, in A.D. 80, it was restored and further embellished.

Toward the end of the eighth century, an order of nuns from Greece established a convent and a small church on the site, naming it *Santa Maria in Minervium*. Five centuries later the Dominicans replaced it with a much larger edifice in the Gothic style. While the utterly plain front hardly suggests a church at all, the interior is reminiscent of the magnificent European cathedrals of the Middle Ages.

A splendid rose window floods the nave with a multicolored sunlight. The walls constitute a museum of Tuscan art with frescoes by Fra Lippo Lippi, Mino da Fiesole and other Renaissance masters.

The floor is a papal cemetery, containing the tombs of five popes: Leo X, Clement VI, Paul IV, Urban VII and Benedict XIII. Under the high altar rests the body of Saint Catherine of Siena.

Less than a hundred meters away along the same street stands the Pantheon, the temple built by Hadrian to honor all the pagan deities. Since A.D. 608, thanks to Pope Boniface IV, the great rotunda has served as the church of *Saint Mary of the Martyrs.*

SANTA MARIA DELLA PACE

A short stroll from the Pantheon, through the picturesque Piazza Navona, brings us to the church of Saint Mary of Peace. Built by Pope Sixtus IV in thanksgiving to the Blessed Virgin for the restoration of peace among the Christian princes of Naples, Florence and Milan in 1482, the church is graced by a unique semi-circular portico by Pietro da Cortona. Its nave ends in an unusual octagonal apse whose side altars mark events in the life of Mary with frescoes by Raphael. Above the main altar are statues representing Peace and Justice by Carlo Maderno. Because of a charming tradition, brides and grooms come here the day after their nuptials to pray for peace in their marriage.

SANTA MARIA IN CAMPITELLI

This lovely Marian church in the heart of old Rome also goes by the name of *Santa Maria in Portico.* In the early sixth century a beautiful young woman named Galla, daughter of a wealthy senator, ran a soup kitchen from the portico of her home on this property, near the Theater of Marcellus, in response to a dream she had one night of the Virgin Mary begging for charity while serving a multitude of the poor and hungry. Galla built a small oratory, Santa Maria in Portico, adjacent to her home. It survived for over a thousand years.

In 1660, Pope Alexander VII invited the architect Rainaldi to raise a new and grander church over Galla's modest chapel. Sometime after her death this devoted servant of the poor was canonized, with October 5 set as her feastday. This Saint Mary's is also acclaimed for an ancient painting of Mary and the Child Jesus displayed above the altar. This likeness of the Virgin Mother and her divine Son was borne in solemn procession throughout the city by Pope Gregory the Great during the plague of 590. The epidemic ceased wherever the painting passed. Here our Lady continues to be invoked as the Protectress of Rome against contagious diseases.

SANTA MARIA IN DOMNICA

The church of Santa Maria in Domnica, on the summit of the Coelian Hill, also has its roots in the sixth century. Recent archeological work indicates that the Marian shrine might have been constructed over and within the remains of a fire station of Imperial Rome.

A stone's throw from another site of early Christian worship, *San Stefano Rotondo*, Santa Maria in Domnica was reconstructed during the pontificate of Paschal I (817–824). Its simple romanesque design is enhanced by a superb arcaded entrance. Two side aisles flank the nave; granite columns hold the triumphal arch that opens onto the sanctuary.

Some Romans call this church *Santa Maria in Navicella* because of the small boat carved in travertine that adorns the piazza out in front. Scholars believe this was placed as a votive offering to Isis, protectress of mariners, whose temple occupied this spot in antiquity.

SANTA MARIA DEL POPOLO

Though condemned to death by the Roman Senate, Nero, when he ended his reign of terror by suicide, was given a full state funeral. His ashes were entombed at the foot of the Pinciana Hill in an elaborate altar of porphyry enclosed by a marble balustrade. Over the ensuing centuries, the people of Rome were spooked by a persistent legend maintaining that the tyrant's ghost haunted the area.

Church of Santa Maria del Santissimo Nome

When Paschal II (1099–1118) ascended the Chair of St. Peter, one of his first acts was to purge the city of "Nero's curse" by destroying the mausoleum and scattering the ashes to the winds. Paschal then established there a church to Mary. In the following century, the structure was enlarged and rendered more splendid with funds from the Romans themselves and renamed Saint Mary of the People.

In subsequent ages the church was favored with exceptional works of art. The right aisle chapel has frescoes painted by Pinturicchio. In a chapel to the left of the sanctuary, Caravaggio placed his masterpieces, the *Conversion of St. Paul* and the *Execution of St. Peter*. The light that floods through the strategically-placed windows enriches the beauty of the interior. The gifted Gian Lorenzo Bernini gave the church its current appearance. This extraordinary church shares the same piazza with two other Marian sanctuaries. Across the vast square, Piazza del Popolo, laid out by the French city planner Valadier in the 1700s, and flanking the Via del Corso, are the identical twin churches of *Santa Maria di Montesanto* and *Santa Maria dei Miracoli*, creations of Rainaldi for Pope Alexander VII (1655–1667). With their porticoes and cupolas and campaniles lending a striking symmetry to the piazza, the twin Saint Marys have long been a favorite of painters and photographers.

These, incidentally, are not the only set of twin Marian churches to be found in Rome. Just off Piazza Venezia, overlooking the rubble of Trajan's Forum, are the look-alike churches of *Santa Maria di Loreto* and *Santissimo Nome di Maria*, both also of the Baroque period.

SANTA MARIA DELLA CONCEZIONE IMMACOLATA

This church stands in the midst of the glamor of the Via Veneto. Cardinal Anton Barberini, twin brother of Pope Urban VIII, erected this church, along with the adjoining monastery, for a community of Capuchin friars. The simple entrance is highlighted by a double staircase; the interior, in keeping with the mendicant way of life, is rather austere.

Beneath the church is one of Rome's most fascinating oddities: five alcoves ornamented with the bones of hundreds of friars. Macabre? Ghoulish? Not at all, say the Capuchin fathers. "This display," they insist, "should be viewed as a solemn but vivid reminder of the swiftness of earthly existence, and as an exhortation to lead a life that will merit the joys of paradise."

SANTA MARIA DELLA VITTORIA

In Piazza San Bernardo near the Acqua Felice Fountain, Pope Paul V had this church constructed to commemorate the victory of Ferdinand II. Ferdinand, with only 25,000 men, routed an army of 100,000 near Prague in 1620. A priest in Ferdinand's forces had held up a small statue of Mary to inspire his comrades as they advanced to the battlefield. Brought to Rome by Gregory XV, the statue is now displayed in the sanctuary here.

The interior of Saint Mary of Victory is among the most luxurious examples of Baroque ornamentation in all of Rome. Bernini's renowned carving—*Saint Teresa in Ecstasy*—draws throngs of art lovers here.

SANTA MARIA IN TRIVIO

A tiny gem that gets its name, as does the Fountain of Trevi, from the piazza it occupies where three narrow streets (*tre vie*) converge, this Saint Mary's has a long and unusual history. Founded in the sixth century by Belisarius, it was erected as an act of penitence for his having exiled Pope Silverius in 537. Belisarius had wrongly suspected the pontiff of having collaborated with the invading Ostrogoths. Silverius, heartbroken and ill, died in solitude on the island of Ponza the following year. A Latin inscription over the doors of the little church recounts all this.

SANTA MARIA EGIZIACA and
SANTA MARIA DEL SOLE

These were both established in the Middle Ages in two still-intact temples from the Republic era of Rome, down in the *Forum Boarium*, the old cattle market.

The local Christian flock had the rectangular Temple of Fortuna Virilis, along the Tiber's right bank, consecrated to Saint Mary of the Egyptians around 880. Built originally by King Servius

Tullius in the sixth century before Christ, the temple was reconstructed under the consuls.

An architectural twin (though smaller) of the Roman temple known as Maison Caree in Nimes in the south of France, this shrine, which has served two religions, remains in an extraordinary state of preservation. Though its travertine stone has darkened with the dust and pollution of the ages, the old edifice still appears majestic, with its high foundation and its front portico of four slender Ionic columns.

Set in the same picturesque little park is the circular church of Saint Mary of the Sun, formerly the Temple of *Mater Matuta* (Goddess of the Dawn). Twenty graceful fluted columns, thirty-two feet tall, ring the rotunda and support the conical tile roof. Built before the Christian era and restored by Vespasian in A.D. 75, this building is alluded to in the writings of Livy: "In the year *Ab Urbe Condita* 456, a quarrel broke out among some matrons near that round temple in the cattle market."

Sometime in the late nineteenth century these two churches were deconsecrated and the structures designated historical sites.

SANTA MARIA IN TRANSPONTINA

The name is derived from its location "across the bridge" from the main part of ancient Rome. It is a relatively young church as the Eternal City reckons time, merely four and a half centuries old.

Saint Mary's Across the Bridge, which is just a short walk down the Via della Conciliazione from St. Peter's Basilica, was built by Pius V (1566–1572). In a side chapel stands a pillar at which Peter the Apostle is said to have been scourged before his crucifixion. On this site, over two thousand years ago, rose a pyramid erected as a monument to Scipio Africanus for crushing Hannibal and his forces on the plains near Carthage in 202 B.C. The church has an impressive high altar crowned by an elegant baldachino, the work of Carlo Fontana. During the Holy Roman Empire it was customary for the emperor-designate and his court to assemble here before starting a formal procession to St. Peter's for the coronation, presided over by the pope.

The campanile houses a great bell that once rang out over the English countryside. It was brought here by English pilgrims in the 1600s.

SANTA MARIA IN COSMEDIN

Even before Caesar's day, there was a Greek settlement in Rome in the *Velabrum* quarter—the low ground between the Tiber and the Circus Maximus. These immigrants continued to practice their ancient pagan rites, raising small shrines here to Zeus and the other Olympic deities.

By the onset of the Middle Ages, however, the Greek community had largely converted to Christianity and had established a deaconry in the neighborhood as a site of Christian worship, calling it *Santa Maria in Schola Greca*. In 782, Pope Adrian I expanded this into a full-sized Romanesque church, after clearing away the decayed remains of the Temple of Ceres and using its stones to construct the apse. The pontiff endowed the edifice with so many mosaics and sculptures and other ornamentations that the Greek word for skill in decorating, *kosmetikos*, was incorporated into the name of the church.

Dimly lit, the interior imparts a general effect of silent, solemn serenity. The marble enclosure of the *Schola Cantorum* (choir), the parallel rows of unmatched columns taken from numerous secular buildings, the faded frescoes high up in the clerestory, the marble canopy over the altar, the graceful apse and the intricate *cosmati* pavement are all a delight to behold. The campanile was added in the eleventh century. Tourists flock to the vestibule of this church to snap photos of the *Bocca della Verità*, the Mouth of Truth. This marble disc, five feet in diameter, adorns the left wall. An ancient cistern cover with a grotesque face carved into it, mouth agape, it is said to be the world's first lie detector. According to legend, anyone putting a hand into the mouth while telling a lie will have the hand bitten off.

SANTA MARIA IN VIA LATA

Founded in the eighth century, this small but attractive church dedicated to Mary is dear to the Roman people. According to a tradition passed down from their distant ancestors, this church incorporates in its foundations parts of the home where St. Paul lived for two years under house arrest. A door on the left of the portico leads down to the subterranean chambers of the first century. Here pilgrims are shown a well said to have been used by Paul to baptize converts. The church claims to possess the bodies of saints Largus, Smaragdus and other martyrs, as well as the head of Saint Cyriacus. Earlier in his priesthood, Pope Pius IX served as canon of the church of Santa Maria in Via Lata.

This is but a sampling of the more than seventy churches in Rome that honor and are named for the Mother of Jesus.

The Roman Catacombs

The early Christians of Rome adopted the ancient Jewish custom of burying their dead in underground cemeteries. Documentary and archeological evidence attest to the existence of a Jewish community in Rome as far back as the second century B.C. Blocked from participation in the economic mainstream of the city, the Jews had to get as much for their meager money as possible in everything they did, including the interment of their dead.

Because of a long-standing law that forbade burial within the city walls, cemeteries were developed outside the gates of Rome along the great roads. Rome's aristocracy would erect imposing family mausolea as repositories for the ashes of their departed. The Jews, early on, discovered that the properties they purchased for burials could be readily tunneled to accommodate a greater number of graves. They found the Roman campagna's subsoil to be of a soft volcanic texture that easily gave way to pick and shovel.

The Jewish people would, at each of these sites, dig an angled shaft about ten feet below the surface, lay out a series of corridors about a yard wide and carve niches into the walls on either side. Into these niches (called *loculi* in Latin) would be placed the bodies of the deceased, having first been wrapped in linen. The tomb would then be closed with a slab of marble, or with bricks or tiles— depending upon what the bereaved family could afford. The slab— or bricks—would then be permanently sealed in place with mortar. An epitaph or some modest identification would then be engraved or painted on the *loculus.*

When they had exhausted every last inch of space in the tunnels, the Jewish workers would dig a shaft in the floor another ten feet down and start another level. Some catacombs have as many as five levels of tunneling. There could be no digging beyond the depth of seventy feet or so, for at that point the volcanic soil ends and gives way to a humid clay texture too difficult to excavate.

Since the first Christian community in Rome took root among the Jews there, it was only logical that it would continue this practice of excavating subterranean cemeteries. One of the earliest of this type of burial ground was situated on the Appian Way, in a low-lying area called *catacumbus* (the hollows). This place eventually gave to all such cemeteries their name.

These places were all dug strictly for interment and not as hiding places, as many romanticized accounts later suggested. It is true, however, that when the church fell under attack at the height of the persecutions, the Christians were forced into more seclusion and secrecy for their liturgical assemblies. At such time, the catacombs were pressed into service as underground churches. There, literally underground, their services would not be disturbed by police raids since all burial grounds were by law inviolable.

At times, however, this law of inviolability was broken by the imperial government in its resolve to annihilate the Christian movement. Emperor Valerian (254–260) was the first to interfere with the religious services in the catacombs. His action led to the Christians' observance of even greater secrecy, the disguising of the approaches to their cemeteries, and even in some instances to the constructing of fake entrances to deceive their tormentors.

The Christian catacombs all came under the jurisdiction of the bishop of Rome. This we learn from ancient documents and inscriptions. Some of the tombs and hallways were adorned with Christian symbols such as the fish, the dove, the olive branch. These were either carved into the stone of the *loculi* or painted on a wall that had first been covered with a layer of stucco. Some of the paintings show clearly that devotion to Mary originated in the earliest times of the church.

Affluent Christians would have a *cubiculum* or small chamber dug out for use as a family crypt. It was in these little rooms that mass would be celebrated in times of great danger. From the late first century to the first few decades of the fourth century, some seventy *coemeteria subterranea* were developed by the faithful of Rome. These ranged from very large cemeteries of nearly a hundred thousand graves, to very small ones of only a few hundred. Most of them were named for a saint or martyr entombed in them.

It was not until after the church was granted full freedom by the Edict of Milan that the use of the catacombs faded. Not long after, the sites became places of pilgrimage. Various popes, especially St. Damasus (366–384), did much to make the old burial grounds accessible to the pilgrims who were now descending on Rome from all over Europe. They caused old staircases to be widened and new ones made, as well as openings to admit air and light from the ground above.

After Rome fell in the late fifth century, the invading hordes of Goths, Vandals and Lombards plundered and desecrated the catacombs. This persuaded later pontiffs to transfer the remains of the martyrs to the Vatican and to numerous churches in the city for greater safety. This herculean task at last completed, the catacombs were closed and abandoned. With the passage of time their entrances and exact locations were forgotten, but in the sixteenth century they began to be rediscovered, often accidentally by workmen toiling in the area and falling into one of the old light shafts. The catacombs once again began to be visited as holy places by both Romans and travelers, as they still are. Presently there are about a dozen of these sites open to public visitation with guided tours. Let us now briefly examine the most important and interesting of these.

THE CATACOMB OF SAINT SEBASTIAN

This cemetery is especially renowned because it is believed that, for a time, the bodies of Peter and Paul were buried here for security during the Emperor Valerian's onslaught against the church. Sebastian, for whom the cemetery was named, was one of the most glorious martyrs of the vicious persecution of Diocletian (see the chapter on St. Sebastian).

Down in these damp, dimly-lit corridors, the visitor gets a

close-up look at the fervor of our forebears. There are hundreds of wall writings by the suffering Christians invoking the intercession of Peter and Paul and other saints. There are religious scenes painted on the walls such as a man in prayer, a shepherd with his flock, and Christ the Savior himself.

The Catacomb of Saint Sebastian spans three levels. The one usually shown to visitors is the middle level, because it is the best preserved.

THE CATACOMB OF DOMITILLA

This is one of the most extensive of Rome's underground cemeteries and one of the oldest, dating to the late first century. Out along the road to the ancient town of Ardea, the Via Ardeatina, Flavia Domitilla, a distant relative of the Emperor Domitian (81–96), had a country villa. Upon embracing the gospel, she gave part of her property for use as a Christian burial ground. Here a catacomb was developed mainly on two levels. These actions resulted in her exile to the desolate island of Ponza, where she lived out her days.

At the beginning of the fourth century, the remains of the martyrs Nereus and Achilleus were placed in a crypt on the newly-dug third level. Pope Damasus (366–384) later expanded this chamber into a miniature basilica to allow for gatherings of pilgrims to celebrate the liturgy here with the priests that escorted them to Rome. Masses are still said here today.

THE CATACOMB OF SANT AGNESE

Dug for the burial of the body of the martyr (A.D. 258) from whom it eventually took its name, this cemetery lies below the Basilica of Saint Agnes on the Via Nomentana, about a mile beyond the walls. Many of the *gallerie* or corridors have remained intact down through the ages, and many of the *loculi* left undisturbed. Thus it affords today's visitor perhaps the most accurate impression of what these cemeteries looked like when they were still operating.

The epitaphs are more legible and instructive in the *Coemeterium Agnetis*, as it was known to the early community.

THE CATACOMB OF THE GIORDANI

Deepest of all of Rome's subterranean cemeteries, this dates to the mid-third century. Its five layers of galleries are richly frescoed in places. Out on the old Salt Road, the Via Salaria, this site is of particular interest because of the burial here of Daria, a Vestal Virgin who, much to the shock and consternation of the imperial authorities, converted to the Christian faith. She and her spouse Crisantus were slain in the persecution of Valerian (257–258). Their bodies were placed in a crypt here, over which a small memorial was later placed. This became a much-venerated spot throughout the Middle Ages. In time, the relics of the two martyrs were transferred to the Basilica dei Santissimi Apostoli.

THE CATACOMB OF PRISCILLA

Also on the Via Salaria, this burial ground was probably named for a daughter of the prominent patrician family of the Acilii. It differs from the other sites in that it was carved out of a pozzolana stone quarry in the third century. On the first level is the so-called *Capella Greca*, Greek Chapel, a rectangular chamber with a frescoed vaulted ceiling. On the archway that divides the nave into two sections is a painting of the Adoration of the Magi, along with the oldest known painting of the Virgin with Child.

THE CATACOMB OF SAINT CALLIXTUS

This site is thought to be the oldest official Christian cemetery of Rome. The renowned catacomb scholar of the nineteenth century, Gian Battista De Rossi, believed this property to have belonged to a family named Cecili. Pope Zephyrinus (199–217) put the deacon Callixtus in charge of this vast burial complex out on the Appian Way. When Callixtus succeeded Zephyrinus to the Chair of St. Peter, he greatly expanded the cemetery. Here great numbers of martyrs were laid to rest, rendering this a particularly sacred site.

Many subsequent popes made it a custom to visit here frequently to pray at the tombs of the martyrs. In fact, at least nine pontiffs of the third century were—at their request—buried here: Pontianus (230-235), Anterus (236), Fabianus (236-250), Lucius I (253-254), Stephen I (254-257), Sixtus II (257-258), Dionysius (259-268), Felix I (269-274) and Eutychian (275-283).

A highlight of a pilgrimage to this catacomb is to gather with the other pilgrims and the guide—usually a Salesian priest or brother—in the *Capella dei Papi*, the chamber where these pontiffs were entombed. The slabs that sealed their *loculi* still bear their engraved names.

Other catacombs that merit a visit by the pilgrim with sufficient time in Rome are those of Commodilla, Pretextatus, and Pamphilius.

The Bishop of Rome

Bishops are the successors of the apostles, both in the authority of their teaching and in the pastoral governance of the church. As successor to St. Peter in the Prince of the Apostle's own see, or diocese, the Bishop of Rome is considered—and has been so considered since the early days of the church—as *primus inter pares*, the first among equals in the College of Bishops. He is, by virtue of the see he occupies, the pope. The Bishop of Rome also bears the following titles: Vicar of Christ on Earth, Archbishop and Metropolitan of the Roman Province, Primate of Italy, Patriarch of the West, Sovereign of Vatican City State, Supreme Pastor of the Universal Church, Pontifex Maximus, and Servant of the Servants of God. The primacy of the pope is real and supreme power not merely a prerogative of honor. He is not just the presiding officer of the collective body of bishops, but truly the head of the church.

From the day Peter himself arrived in Rome—somewhere around the year A.D. 42, tradition says—the Eternal City has been the residence of the popes, except for the first three quarters of the fourteenth century when seven of them, from Clement V to Gregory XI, chose to lead the church from Avignon in southern France. Since the return of Gregory XI in 1377, the popes have dwelled in Rome.

Today, visitors to Rome may see the successor to St. Peter on two occasions each week. On Wednesdays, the Holy Father holds his weekly public audience. In the warm months, from May to September, this takes place in St. Peter's Square. The rest of the year, audiences are held in the modern Paul VI Audience Hall, to the left of the Basilica. At these gatherings, the pope delivers a lengthy talk on some current issue concerning the church or the world at large. He speaks in Italian, since that is the language of his Roman flock. Tickets for these audiences can be obtained from the office of the *Prefecture of the Apostolic Household* in the Vatican, or by writing to the *Casa Santa Maria*, Via Dell'Umilita, 30, Rome, Italy 00187.

The other regular weekly public appearance of the pope is at his window, in the Apostolic Palace overlooking St. Peter's Square, at noon on Sunday. On this occasion, he leads the recitation of the Angelus and then gives a brief spiritual message. Tickets are not required for this.

On Christmas Day and Easter Sunday, at 12 noon following the pontifical mass, the Holy Father appears on the central balcony of St. Peter's Basilica to impart the special blessing called *Urbi et Orbi*, to the City and to the World.

Visitors seeking to have religious articles blessed by the pope need only to hold them in their hands when he closes each of his public appearances with his benediction. Often a monsignor assisting the pope will announce just beforehand: "The Holy Father will now impart his apostolic blessing upon all of you and upon any religious articles you have brought with you for that purpose."

The Holy Stairs

Rome is renowned for, among other things, its profusion of
elegant flights of marble stairs—some indoors, leading to
staterooms in Renaissance mansions, others outdoors,
climbing to churches or descending one or another of the city's
fabled seven hills. Only one of all these staircases, however, is known
as "holy."

Diagonally across the piazza from the Basilica of St. John Lateran is a two-story, gray sandstone structure that enshrines *La Scala
Santa*, a flight of twenty-eight marble steps that tradition claims
once led to the office of Pontius Pilate in Jerusalem. Soon after her
conversion to Christianity in the early fourth century, Helena, the
mother of Constantine, set out for the province of Judea to gather
things that were touched by Christ, including the "True Cross."
Inferring that Christ must have ascended these stairs for his arraign-
ment before the provincial governor and descended them en route
to Golgotha, Helena had them dismantled and shipped to Rome.

Upon its arrival in Rome, the staircase was placed on the right
of the entrance to the Lateran Palace, which had become by that
time the official papal residence. This tradition is supported by the
fact that the steps are cut from a type of marble commonly used in
Jerusalem at that time, and by reports in later centuries confirming
that the steps to the formal entrance of the governor's palace were
missing.

Known throughout the Middle Ages as the *Scala Pilati*, the
staircase was the object of veneration and the setting for many papal
processions. These things are mentioned in the *Liber Pontificalis*,
written in the sixth century, which contains the biographies of the
popes. In 1589, having carried out extensive alterations to the Lateran Palace, Pope Sixtus V had the stairs moved to their present
site where they serve as the ceremonial approach to the papal chapel
called *Sancta Sanctorum*, or Holy of Holies. This small oratory, so

named because of the great number of relics it houses, was built during the pontificate of Nicholas III (1277-1289). Most of the relics and their reliquaries date back to the first few centuries of Christianity. On the frieze above the altar are engraved these words:

> NON EST IN TOTO
> SANCTIOR ORBE LOCUS
> (In the whole world there is no holier place.)

Firmly believing that these steps had indeed been sanctified by the feet of Christ, pontiffs since Sixtus V have ascended them on their knees on every visit to the Sancta Sanctorum. Seeking to encourage public veneration of the Holy Stairs by personal example, Pope Clement VIII made the ascent on more than a hundred occasions in the Jubilee Year of 1600. Some later popes who practiced this devotion were Urban VIII (1623-1644), Innocent X (1644-1655) and Clement X (1670-1676).

Pius IX (1846-1878) had Ignazio Iacometti, a leading sculptor of the time, set up two of his most acclaimed works on either side of the bottom of the Scala Santa: *Christ Receiving the Kiss of Judas* and *Christ Presented to the Rabble by Pontius Pilate*, also called *Ecce Homo*. In 1853, Pius entrusted the care of the sanctuary to the Passionist Fathers, who have remained in charge to the present day.

From the Jubilee of 1600 on, tens of thousands of devout Romans and pilgrims to the Eternal City have made the arduous climb on their knees, pausing on each step to pray and meditate on the sufferings of Jesus. This devotion is still favored by pilgrims, and it is an inescapably moving experience, regardless of one's beliefs, to witness throngs of the faithful moving slowly up the dimly-lit staircase and to hear the murmur of their prayers. It is an essential stop for any pilgrim visiting Rome for the Holy Year A.D. 2000.

Good Friday and
the Colosseum

One of the best known and most photographed sights in the world is the Colosseum of Rome. This enormous relic of imperial times was begun by the Emperor Vespasian in A.D. 72 and completed by his son Titus in A.D. 80. The arena was given the official title of Amphitheatrum Flavianum, the Flavian Amphitheater, for the family name of the two emperors.

Designed as a stadium for spectacles featuring gladiators and wild beasts, the Colosseum (so called by the general public because of its colossal size) is elliptical, measuring 188 meters on its greater axis by 156 meters on the smaller. Its outer walls reached a height of 57 meters. The wall consisted of three arcades in the three Greek orders. The ground floor arches were flanked by Doric columns, the second and third levels by Ionic and Corinthian columns respectively. The interior was composed of a brick substructure that supported tier upon tier of marble grandstands. Boasting a seating capacity of 50,000, the Colosseum had an ingenious system of corridors and stairwells that admitted every spectator directly to his numbered seat.

Beneath the floor of the stadium was a series of hallways, off of which were locker rooms, storage rooms and cages. The combatants—human and otherwise—were brought up to the field of combat by a system of rope-driven elevators. Over all the seating sections stretched canvas awnings to shelter the crowd from the blistering Mediterranean sun or a sudden rainshower. The floor could even be flooded for mock naval battles. Except for such occasions, the floor of tightly-fitted planks was covered with a heavy layer of sand (in Latin, *arena*—hence our generic name for any stadium today).

Records show that the Colosseum was still totally intact and

The Colosseum

in use until the seventh century. Soon after, however, it fell into abandonment and decay, its huge slabs of marble and travertine often carried away by Rome's nobility for their villas, monuments and palaces.

Fortunately, Pius VII (1800–1823) put a stop to this, or we would not even have what remains today. Subsequent popes took steps to continue the preservation of this massive ruin, thought to be part of the history of the early church. Tradition has long maintained that Christians were martyred here by the thousands. To commemorate their suffering, at midfield there now stands a huge wooden cross. In chapter twenty-three of *Fabiola*, Cardinal Nicholas Wiseman describes his feelings upon visiting the Colosseum for the first time:

> In the arena where we now stand, Christian martyrs once knelt, their eyes fixed on the ground while the pagan mob awaited with impatience the shedding of their blood, and yelled in

maddening excitement: "The Christians to the lions!" Tender virgins once knelt there, young men too, and boys of noble aspect, with their gaze fixed on Heaven, fearless in the midst of that sea of human passions, undismayed by the roars of the savage beasts pacing in their dens close by.

What a spectacle it was, savage and sublime! The rays of a brilliant sun inundated the vast edifice with its light; marbles, columns, statues—all were resplendent. The awning with its graceful undulations cooled the scorching rays of the sun and tempered its brilliance. A sacrifice to Jupiter is first offered in the presence of the Emperor. Then the signal is given for another sacrifice. It is not Caesar, but a young girl, one of the Vestal Virgins, who rises and gives the sign. At once the cages encircling the area are opened and with bounds as if of joy at regaining their liberty, the savage beasts, not yet heeding their victims, traverse the whole space again and again. One tiger pauses, its attention arrested. Suddenly all the animals are motionless. They then advance stealthily at first as if in fear. A bound! And the martyr's soul is in the embrace of his God.

On Good Friday night, by centuries-old custom, the pope leads the *Via Crucis*, the Stations of the Cross, along the Via Fori Imperiali, which culminates in a prayer vigil inside the floodlit Colosseum. It is one of the most dramatic, powerful, and unforgettable pageants a pilgrim can witness: the Supreme Pontiff in meditation where the flock of Peter agonized, where Roman tyrants sought to drown the infant church in its own blood.

The Pantheon: Hadrian's Masterpiece

L ooming over a quaint piazza down in the heart of the old Campus Martius is the most *durable* of architectural treasures bequeathed to us by Imperial Rome: the Pantheon, temple to all the gods. Unlike the Forum, the Colosseum and the aqueducts, it is not a ruin. Rather, it sits virtually intact, unimpaired by nearly two thousand years' exposure to man, time and the elements. Erected in 27 B.C. by Augustus' prime minister, Agrippa, the Pantheon was destroyed by fire. Around A.D. 126 it was rebuilt by the Emperor Hadrian. The original inscription is still to be seen on the frieze of the portico: *M. Agrippa L. F. Cos. Tertium Fecit*—Built by Marcus Agrippa, son of Lucius, in his third consulship.

The Pantheon, also known as Church of St. Mary of the Martyrs

Hadrian, a gifted amateur architect, undertook the construction of a domed rotunda on a lavish scale. Today the exterior is denuded of much of its splendor. Gone are the bas-reliefs that once adorned the pediment. Gone too is the facing of travertine marble. The interior, however, comes down to us much as Hadrian knew it. The spacious entrance portico has a grove of sixteen columns, each a granite monolith of pinkish gray crowned by a Corinthian capital. The two large recesses flanking the colossal doors originally housed statues of Augustus and Agrippa. They now stand empty.

The doors are among the most astonishing of all Roman relics. They were standing in ages past as toga-clad emperors, senators, and Roman society went by. In our day they admit hordes of camera-toting tourists from far-off lands. Having passed through the bronze doors which still pivot on their original hinges, the visitor steps into a truly noble hall studded with niches once graced by colossal statues of the seven planetary deities. These recesses now contain sculptures of the Virgin Mary and various saints. Also found here in our time are the tombs of Italy's first two kings and that of the Renaissance genius, Raphael.

One's eyes are drawn upward to the breathtaking coffered dome and ultimately to the *oculus*, an opening in the roof twenty-seven feet in diameter, which provided the only light and air for the windowless building. Symbolically, it allowed the gods to look down from the heavens into the temple raised in their honor. There's still more symbolism to be found here. The temple is a perfect sphere— 133 feet in diameter and the same in height. If the circumference of the dome were continued it would form a ball just touching the center of the floor. This roundness represents the eternalness of the Roman gods. The coffered dome was meant to resemble the vault of the sky, the abode of the gods. The very name of the temple, *Pantheon*, is Greek for "all gods." The building was the Romans' eloquent way of exalting the divine quality in everything that exists.

Through the *oculus* pours the light of day, illuminating the whole of this vast, wondrous hall. It is thrilling to stand here on a showery day and watch the rain cascade through in one great circular shaft that brings to mind a fluted column. Cleverly concealed drains in the convex floor prevent puddling. The beautiful tiled pavement is the same one that felt the sandals of the Caesars and their subjects. It is inlaid with porphyry, gray granite and different marbles from Asia and Africa, and gleams with striking colors.

High above soars the dome. The arch was borrowed from the Etruscans, the three orders—of Doric, Ionic, and Corinthian—from the Greeks. But the dome was a Roman contrivance, introduced in the second century B.C. after the development of concrete or stiffly-mortared rubble. The earliest surviving example of the Roman dome is in the *frigidarium* of the Stabian Baths at Pompeii. The diameter of the vault is just a few feet more than that of the cupola of St. Peter's Basilica, making it the largest in the world. Coincidentally, the bronze that once veneered the exterior of the Pantheon's dome was peeled off in 1630, by direction of the architect master Bernini, for the canopy over the papal altar in St. Peter's.

There is a fascinating story that comes to us across the ages of how the ancient builders were able to raise the great dome. It is said that the entire interior of the temple was filled tight with topsoil, culminating in an enormous mound in the shape of the dome. The authorities had ordered mixed into the soil hundreds of thousands of gold coins. When the mortar of the dome set, the public was invited in to clear the Pantheon of the dirt, and to keep for themselves any coins they unearthed in the process. Within a day or two, the rotunda was emptied of soil and ready for offering worship to all the gods.

This best preserved of the monuments of ancient Rome owes its remarkable condition to the fact that in A.D. 609 it was consecrated as a Christian church by Pope Boniface IV, with the permission of the Byzantine Emperor Phocas. It has been a church ever since, under the name of St. Mary and the Martyrs, and has consequently been carefully maintained.

A sojourn in Rome would hardly be complete without a visit to the Pantheon. There is a mystical calm here, a sacred repose which soothes and elevates and refreshes. There truly is in the Pantheon a sense of the divine quality in everything that exists—a sense of awe, solemnity and eternity.

The Mamertine

Lasciate ogni speranza, voi ch' entrate! "Abandon all hope, ye who enter here!" Thus reads the sign over the gates of hell, the poet Dante informs us. The same inscription would have been appropriate above the entrance to ancient Rome's Mamertine Prison. Few, if any, inmates of that grotesque institution ever saw the light of day again. If they did, it was while being dragged to their execution.

Just outside the great Forum, and in marked contrast to its temples, law courts and monuments of gleaming white marble, stood the dark, foreboding, squalid subterranean jail. Carved out of the volcanic rock at the foot of the Capitoline Hill by order of Ancus Martius, fourth king of Rome (640–616 B.C.), the dreaded Mamertine was to serve as the principal prison of the Eternal City for more than a thousand years.

Beneath the jail, the sixth king, Servius Tullius, (578–535 B.C.) excavated an even more hideous chamber which took its name from him, the Tullianum Dungeon. The early Roman historian Sallust describes the lower level thus: "There is a place in the prison which is called the Tullianum. It is about twelve feet deep in the ground. Its appearance is disgusting and vile by reason of the filth, the darkness, and the stench." Dispensing with the most basic amenities, the king never bothered to construct a staircase descending into the airless dungeon. The only entrance was through a hole in the stone floor of the upper jail. Prisoners condemned to be strangled or starved to death were thrown down through the opening.

This dank and dismal hellhole measured six and a half feet high, thirty feet long, and twenty-two feet wide. The far wall had an iron door (still visible) that opened into the *Cloaca Maxima*, or main sewer, which ran under the prison on its way to the Tiber. On some occasions bodies of the executed were disposed of through this door. The steps which led from the citadel high upon the Capitoline down to the prison were known as the *Scalae Gemoniae*, or the Staircase of Sighs. Like the Bridge of Sighs in Venice, the steps were so named because the shackled prisoners descending them, knowing they were doomed, would sigh at their last view of the world. These marble steps were also used for displaying the bodies of some executed prisoners before they were tossed into the river. Suetonius, another of the early historians, writes: "Those who were put to death were exposed on the staircase and then hauled off to the Tiber."

The Roman scholar Pliny relates a pathetic story that suggests the many touching scenes which must have occurred there:

> In the reign of Tiberius, when the bodies of Titus Sabinus and his servants were exposed, one of them was watched over by his dog. The affectionate animal was seen to bring some bread which it had stolen and attempt to force it into the mouth of its dead master. These men were victims of Sejanus, whose own body was erelong flung down upon the same accursed place.

Sejanus, principal adviser to Tiberius, was one of a long list of celebrated figures in Roman history who breathed their last within the foul walls of the Tullianum. The German general Vercingetorix, who defied Julius Caesar in Gaul, was strangled here. So, too, was Simon Bar Jioras, defender of Jerusalem when Titus captured the city and destroyed the temple in A.D. 70. When the allies of the Roman conspirator Catiline—Lentulus, Cethegus, Gabinius, Statilius and Ceparius—were put to death in the dungeon on December fifth, 63 B.C., Cicero mounted the Staircase of Sighs and announced the prisoners' demise to the waiting crowd thus: *Vixerunt!* ("They have lived!").

But certainly the most celebrated inmates of the Mamertine were the apostles Peter and Paul in A.D. 66. Tradition maintains that the two Christian leaders were confined in the nightmarish Tullianum for nine months during Nero's reign of terror. The same tradition holds that they continued to preach even here, converting their wardens Processus and Martinianus along with forty fellow prisoners to the teachings of Christ, to which they all bore witness through torture and death. In the prison there was no water with which to baptize the new converts. But it is said that a miraculous spring welled up out of the rocky ground.

Of course, there can be no doubt that a multitude of less renowned men—criminals and innocents alike—languished here in misery and perished in abysmal darkness. In all the world surely there is no other room of such modest size that is so imbued with black memories and horrors. Even today the visitor finds that the Mamertine and the Tullianum—their every stone drenched in blood—evoke all the human suffering that took place here.

In both the upper and lower chambers small altars have been installed for the celebration of mass. The whole prison complex is also known as the church of *San Pietro in Carcere*.

The Madonna Shrines

The Roman people's love for and devotion to Mary is everywhere evident in the Eternal City. Almost sixty of the city's churches are named for her. Many homes display a painting of the Blessed Mother. Many courtyards feature a statue of her.

There are also hundreds of *Madonelle*, statuettes of the Madonna, in niches on the fronts of buildings—especially corner buildings. Some are simple and unadorned, others ornamental—yet always tasteful. The best of these date from the Baroque period when they were decorated with stucco and wrought iron. This practice goes back to medieval times. The local *Madonella* was a neighborhood's way of invoking the blessing and protection of the Virgin Mary. When the Angelus bells rang out at eventide, votive oil lamps were placed before these miniature shrines. These lamps helped to light Rome's streets in the days before public electric illumination. As late as the end of the eighteenth century, more than two thousand of these Madonelle graced the office buildings and apartment houses of Rome. Some fifteen hundred have survived to our time, as a walk through the city, particularly the old districts, will reveal.

Many of the shrines are additionally adorned with silver hearts engraved with the letters P.G.R.—*per grazie ricevute* (for favors received). These are thank-you offerings to the Blessed Mother for her intercession during some family crisis or the like. One is often greeted with a similar sight in the little dimly-lit stores and shops in the back alleys of Rome. In the background or in a corner there is often a small niche occupied by an image of the Virgin, before which burns a votive candle, glowing with quiet devotion. Lights in front of such Madonelle often also burn in the antechamber of a prince or count or cardinal. In the living room of the working man, too, such shrines are frequently found. Each evening the mother of such a household gathers the family for prayer in the peaceful gleam of the flickering candle illuminating the face of Mary.

Rome enthusiastically celebrates every great feast of the Blessed Mother, especially the Assumption on August 15, with illuminated statues and paintings of the Mother of Christ. On Sunday afternoons, in years gone by, some devout Romans would walk the streets and offer a *Hail Mary* at every Madonella they came upon, until they had said five decades of the Rosary.

Clearly, Mary remains the patroness of the eternal city of Rome.

Christianity and
Secular Rome

Rome is truly beautiful and owes much of its embellishment to the popes, the cardinals, and other church figures. Pilgrims in search of Christianity's stamp on secular Rome will observe the term *PONTIFEX MAXIMUS*, or its abbreviated form *PONT MAX*, all over town.

In the year A.D. 410 Alaric marched on Rome. The once vaunted imperial capital was now at the mercy of its many attackers. In 452 Attila and his Huns stormed the gates. Three years later the Vandals plundered the city for a fortnight. In 476 the mighty Roman Empire—after a long terminal illness of decadence, depravity and corruption—at last succumbed. Through it all, the church remained the refuge of order and culture. The population of Rome itself dwindled from a million and a half to a mere fifteen thousand beleaguered souls who, in the absence of a local government, were forced to fend for themselves against brigands, pestilence, famine and despair. They began to turn more and more to the only remaining viable institution in their midst—the church. Thus it was that the head of the church, the Bishop of Rome, began to exercise temporal as well as spiritual power in the city on the Tiber.

Throughout the Middle Ages and the period of the Renaissance, and up to the mid-nineteenth century, the church, through the papacy, left its imprint everywhere on secular Rome—preserving the ancient ruins, restoring the old aqueducts, crowning with the Cross of Christ each of the obelisks brought back from Egypt by Caesar's legions, commissioning new fountains and laying out new streets and squares. Most of the city's spectacular fountains bear this stamp, along with the familiar symbols of the papacy: the tiara and the crossed keys. The inscriptions are always in Latin.

It was the church leaders that got the old aqueducts running again, bringing water in from distant points in every direction. Each of these pipelines ends in a *terminus* fountain of exceptional splendor, nourishing numerous less-elaborate fountains along the way. The *Fontana Paolina* high up on the Janiculum Hill is one such *terminus*. Named for the pope who commissioned it, Paul V, it roars with five cascades pouring into a vast basin. The entablature informs us that the water comes from Lake Bracciano north of Rome, and that it is pure and excellent for one's health. Also engraved on the facade are these words:

> PAULUS QUINTUS PONTIFEX MAXIMUS
> ANNO DOMINI MDCX II
> PONTIFICATUS SUI SEPTIMO

Paul V, Chief Priest, in the year of our Lord 1612, the seventh (year) of his pontificate.

Down in the heart of the city, a district Caesar knew as the *Campus Martius*, the fabled *Fontana di Trevi*, Trevi Fountain, bears on high the name of two later successors of St. Peter:

> CLEMENS XII PONT MAX
> ANNO DOMINI MD CCXXXV PONTIF VI
> PERFECIT BENEDICTUS XIV PONT MAX

(Begun under) Clement XII, Chief Priest in the year of our Lord 1735, sixth (year) of his pontificate. Completed by Benedict XIV, Chief Priest.

On the summit of the Quirinal Hill is a street named *Via delle Quattro Fontane*, because of the fountains on all the corner buildings where it intersects with *Via Venti Settembre*. These bear the stamp of that tireless city planner, Pope Sixtus V.

Many of the magnificent edifices that make Rome an architectural wonderland are also the products of church figures. The Palazzo Venezia, built in 1450 for Cardinal Pietro Barbo, who became Pope Paul II, later served as the seat of the Austro-Hungarian Embassy to the Holy See. The fortress-like palace is remembered today mostly for its use as the headquarters of Mussolini's fascist government in the 1930s and early 1940s. It is now a repository of art and historical collections.

The *Palazzo Farnese* was begun in 1514 by Antonio da Sangallo and completed by Michelangelo for Cardinal Alessandro Farnese, later Pope Paul III. It serves today as the seat of the French Embassy to the Vatican.

The *Palazzo della Cancelleria*, with its magnificent courtyard, is the seat of the Pontifical Chancellor—the chancery office of the Rome diocese. Perched on the ridge of the Janiculum Hill overlooking St. Peter's is the Pontifical North American College, America's seminary in Rome. Back in 1855, Pope Pius IX urged the bishops of the United States to open a seminary here so that promising young men could study for the priesthood in the inspiring ambience of the See of St. Peter, in that "unique classroom called Rome," as Pius IX put it. The original building of the college, still in use, is the *Casa Santa Maria* on the *Via dell'Umilta* near the Trevi Fountain. This is now used for housing priests doing graduate work in theology and other ecclesiastical fields of study. The spacious modern facility on the Janiculum was dedicated by Pope Pius XII on October 14, 1953. U. S. bishops usually reside here during their *ad limina* visits and other trips to Rome.

Many American priests and seminarians also study at other sites in Rome, such as the Pontifical Gregorian University (affectionately called the "Greg" by the students), and the Pontifical University of St. Thomas Aquinas, also known as the *Angelicum*.

Even the main outdoor produce market in the *Campo dei Fiori* shows evidence that Rome is a Christian city. High over the stalls, with their immense canvas umbrellas, stands the statue of the monk, Saint Bruno. The hand of the church can also be observed in many charitable institutions throughout the city. Numerous hospitals that still serve the Romans and their visitors are the creations of various popes, some as far back as Medieval and Renaissance times. The oldest hospital in the Eternal City is the *Ospedale di Santo Spirito*.

In the eighth century, King Ina of the Anglo-Saxons founded a pilgrims' lodging house for his countrymen in the Borgo quarter near the Tiber. Pope Innocent III, in 1201, converted and expanded this into a hospital for pilgrims. Two beautiful churches stand on either corner of this block-long structure: *Santo Spirito in Sassia* and *Santa Maria in Sassia*. The words *in Sassia* mean "in the Saxon quarter of the city."

The city's several triumphal arches bear witness not only to the grandeur that once was Rome, but also to the victory of Christianity over paganism. These grand marble archways were a popular form of Roman monument, usually erected to glorify successes on the battlefield. The oldest is the Arch of Titus, which celebrated that ruler's conquests in Palestine. An inscription on the northern face reminds those who appreciate antiquities that they owe a debt of gratitude to Pope Pius VII for his rescue of Titus' monument from centuries of debris, and for its fine restoration in 1823.

In A.D. 315, the senate erected the Arch of Constantine, still standing just a few meters from the Colosseum. Featuring a collage of reliefs stripped from earlier works, such as the Arch of Trajan, it hails the victories of the first Christian emperor. From a lofty perch on the upper façade, imperial statues gaze at the street below. If they could speak they would provide us with stirring eyewitness accounts of the armies that fought around the monument's base— from the Huns, the Goths, the Lombards, the Swiss Guards, the Brown Shirts of Mussolini, the goose-stepping Nazis of Hitler, to the liberating American forces advancing from Anzio in June of 1943.

Christianity's symbol, the cross, crowns Rome's numerous obelisks. These towering stone shafts were brought back from Egypt by the conquering legions of the Caesars. In the land of the pharaohs, these monoliths of granite stood before temples and palaces and were associated with the worship of the sun. In the Eternal City today, their hieroglyphics still legible, the obelisks serve as focal points of numerous piazzas. The most exquisite of these "exclamation points," as some Romans call them, is the one in St. Peter's Square. Climbing a hundred feet into the Vatican sky, the obelisk is surmounted by an iron cross said to contain a fragment of the true Cross. Pope Sixtus V had these words inscribed on the pedestal: *Ecce Crucem Domini. Christus Vincit. Christus regnat. Christus imperat.* Behold the Cross of the Lord. Christ conquers. Christ reigns. Christ rules.

Honorary columns left over from imperial days also proclaim the ubiquitous presence of Christianity in the city on the Tiber. Out of the rubble of the Forum rises a one-hundred-and-forty-foot-high shaft of Carrara marble. Vivid bas-reliefs exalting Trajan's military accomplishments wind their way from the bottom to the top, where a small platform once held a statue of the emperor. Since 1586, however, a carving of St. Peter holding the "Keys to the Kingdom" has occupied this lofty perch, his gaze fixed out over the rooftops on the distant dome of his basilica. A few blocks away, Saint Paul's likeness stands atop a similar column that was erected to honor the philosopher-emperor, Marcus Aurelius.

With the decline and fall of the old empire, a number of the gates that pierce the third-century Aurelian Walls were renamed for Christian saints. The Aurelian Gate became *Porta San Pancrazio;* the Prenestine Gate became *Porta San Lorenzo.* Saints John, Paul and Sebastian also had entrance ways named for them: *Porta San Giovanni, Porta San Paolo* and *Porta San Sebastiano.*

About a mile and a half upstream from Rome's *Porta del Popolo*, the Milvian Bridge still carries the Via Flaminia over the Tiber and sends it on its way to northeastern Italy. Legend claims that it was on this bridge that Constantine had a vision of the Cross in the sky, encircled with the words *In Hoc Signo Vinces*—In this sign you shall conquer. Built by the consul Amelius Scaurus a hundred years before the birth of Christ, the *Pons Milvius* is graced at one end by statues of the Savior and John the Baptist, and at the other end by figures of the Virgin Mother and St. John Nepomycene.

Just a few yards away, on the far bank of the river, stands the Church of the Holy Cross, commissioned by Pope Pius X in 1912 to mark the sixteen-hundredth anniversary of the apparition that changed Rome and the world forever. Downstream a few miles, also on the opposite bank from the main part of the city, stands one of the architectural wonders of second-century Rome, the Tomb of Hadrian. This massive mausoleum also bears the imprint of Christianity, as does the ancient bridge leading to it.

One night in 590, Pope Gregory the Great led a solemn procession through the city toward St. Peter's, imploring God to end the plague that was daily claiming hundreds of his flock. When Gregory arrived at the *Pons Aelius*, he beheld an angel sheathing his sword atop the imperial sepulcher. The following day the pestilence lifted. To commemorate this blessing, the pontiff placed a statue of Michael the Archangel on the spot where the apparition had occurred. Ever since, the Roman people have referred to the structure as *Castel Sant'Angelo.*

Toward the end of his reign, Pope Clement VII placed statues of Peter and Paul at the entrance to the bridge. In the 1600s Bernini and his students added ten travertine angels to the balustrade and renamed the span "The Bridge of Angels." Further down stream on the plain along the Tiber, and just barely within the Aurelian Walls, rises *Monte Testaccio*, an elevation formed by broken earthenware vessels (*testae* in Latin) discarded over centuries from the nearby docks. In the Middle Ages this served as Golgotha for Good Friday pageants reenacting Christ's trek along Jerusalem's Via Dolorosa. Today, Testaccio is topped by a tall iron cross as a reminder of that solemn custom.

Indeed, wherever pilgrims to Rome walk—whether up on the seven hills and in their many parks, or down in the teeming squares and bustling streets—they will be reminded again and again that Rome is truly the seat of Christendom, the See of St. Peter, the heart of the Catholic Church, and the home of the pope.

In the Footsteps
of the Saints

During the turbulent reigns of emperors Claudius and Nero, two Jewish strangers from Syria arrived in Rome— one a fisherman from Galilee, the other a tentmaker from Tarsus. They came to disseminate the simple message of a prince of peace. They found a populace that worshiped many deities who were believed to control all things dear to mortals—life, health and prosperity. Every day, every hour, every act of terrestrial existence was associated with thoughts of celestial divinities whose province and privilege it was to foster—or hinder—all the plans of earthly beings.

In their relentless and fearless preaching of the "Good News," Peter and Paul began slowly but surely to alter the face, the character, the very soul of a city that was already known as "Eternal." Since then, two thousand years of Christian pilgrims have made their way to Rome in a fervent desire to deepen their faith through praying at the tombs of the apostles and martyrs.

Today's pilgrims walk in the footsteps of scores of holy men and women long since raised to the altars of the Church Triumphant in heaven. Among the saints who felt a special attraction to Rome we find: Aloysius Gonzaga, Bernardino of Siena, Catherine of Siena, Ambrose, Augustine, Jerome, Philip Neri, Charles Borromeo, Cyril and Methodius, Dominic and Francis, Thomas of Canterbury, Wilfrid of York, John of Matha, Felix de Valois, Odo of Cluny, Nilus, Martin I, Malachy, Anselm, Alphonse Ligouri, Francis Xavier, Monica, Catherine of Sweden, Bridget of Sweden, Ignatius of Loyola, Camillus de Lellis, Cajetan, John Berchmans, Stanislaus Kostka—to name but a few.

Neither the difficulties of the journey, nor even the danger of death, have deterred men and women across the centuries from their dream of seeing Rome. In 269 St. Marcius came with his wife Martha and their two sons all the way from Persia. St. Paternus traveled from Alexandria in 253, St. Maerus from Africa in 284. When Saints Constantine and Victorian reached Rome they went at once to the tomb of St. Peter, where soldiers caught them and put them to death. St. Zoe was found praying at the same holy site and immediately martyred. Each one of them discovered these timeless truths: a pilgrimage to Rome moves one profoundly and changes one's view of life forever. More than anywhere else, this is the place to strengthen one's faith and increase one's devotion. Simple experiences here are never forgotten—such as walking to Sunday mass to the sweet sound of church bells throughout the city. Extraordinary experiences, like celebrating the sacred mysteries down in the catacombs, repeat themselves over and over in the mind's eye years after a Roman pilgrimage. Receiving the Eucharist in churches whose stones were laid in apostolic times is a spiritual joy beyond the power of words to convey.

Today's pilgrims will come inexorably to the same conclusion of the untold millions of kings and queens, bishops and priests, nuns, and laypeople that preceded them—namely, that this incomparably enchanting city of oleanders and pines, palaces and fountains, monuments and balconies, and the majestic debris of imperial days, is first and foremost the seat of Christendom—and has been so ever since the apostles from Syria planted the Cross of Christ here.

In his *Tractate on the Jubilee of 1575*, Saint Peter Canisius, a Jesuit priest, told of the many treasures Rome has to offer the pilgrim:

> Before his eyes stretches the city where the principal apostles preached the Gospel, the streets which the holy martyrs trod and hallowed with their blood, the churches they continue to adorn with their relics. Who would not be moved at visiting the sites where Peter was crucified, Paul beheaded, and John cast into boiling oil, where Peter asked of Christ, "Lord, whither goest Thou?"

Who would not deepen his faith standing at the tombs of
Laurence and Sebastian, praying in the house churches of Agnes
and Cecilia and Prisca, climbing the steps from Pilate's house
that felt the feet of Christ in the time of his bitter passion?

One of the most dominant and nagging thoughts a first-time
visitor to Rome will have is: "When is the soonest I can return?"
For in its totality, Rome—especially Christian Rome—is inex-
haustible. Claire Booth Luce, former United States ambassador to
Italy and a convert to Catholicism, put it this way: "To grasp Rome
one would require the eye of Michelangelo, the mind of Aquinas,
the soul of Dante, the resolve of Caesar, and the lifespan of
Methusaleh. It would then take a hundred large volumes to describe
the experience."

This is merely one small volume, but it is a start. Confucius
noted that even a journey of a thousand miles still must begin with
the first step. It is my hope that this book will prove to be of some
help to the reader in taking that first step toward knowing Immortal Rome and understanding its unending role in the dramatic story
of Christianity.

National Churches

Pilgrims of various nationalities can find churches in Rome where they can attend mass and hear a homily in their native language. Here is a brief directory of such churches:

Americans	Santa Susanna
English	San Silvestro in Capite
Scottish	Sant Andrea degli Scozzesi
French	San Luigi dei Francesi
German	Santa Maria dell'Anima
Irish	Sant Agata dei Goti
Polish	Sant Stanislao
Portuguese	Sant Antonio dei Portoghesi
Romanian	San Salvatore in Lauro
Spanish	Santa Maria di Monserrato
Czech	San Girolamo degli Schiavoni
Hungarian	San Stefano Rotondo

People of Catholic rites, other than Latin, may also attend a liturgy to which they are accustomed.

Armenian	San Nicola da Tolentino
Greek	Sant Atanasio
Maronite	San Marone
Russian-Slavonic	San Lorenzo dei Monti
Russian	Sant Antonio in Esquilino

Addresses of Rome's Churches and Catacombs

S. Agata dei Goti	Via Mazzarino
S. Agnese in Agone	Piazza Navonna
S. Agostino	Piazza S. Agostino
S. Anastasia	Piazza S. Anastasia
S. Andrea al Quirinale	Via del Quirinale, 29
S. Andrea della Valle	Piazza Vidoni
S. Angelo in Pescheria	Via del Portico d'Ottavia
SS. Apostoli	Piazza SS. Apostoli
S. Bartolomeo	Isola Tiberina
S. Carlo al Corso	Via del Corso 437
S. Cecilia	Piazza S. Cecilia
S. Clemente	Via Labicana, 95
SS. Cosma e Damiano	Via dei Fori Imperiali, 1
S. Costanza	Via Nomentana, 349
S. Crisogono	Piazza Sonnino
S. Croce	Piazza S. Croce
S. Francesca Romana	Foro Romano
Il Gesù	Piazza del Gesù
S. Giorgio in Velabro	Via del Velabro, 19
S. Giovanni a Porta Latina	Via di Porta Latina, 17
SS. Giovanni e Paolo	Piazza SS Giovanni e Paolo
S. Gregorio	Via S. Gregorio I
S. Ignazio	Piazza S. Ignazio
S. Lorenzo in Damaso	Piazza della Cancelleria
S. Lorenzo Fuori Le Mura	Piazzale del Verano, 3
S. Lorenzo in Panisperna	Via Panisperna
SS. Luca e Martino	Via della Curia, 8
S. Luigi dei Francesi	Piazza S. Luigi dei Francesi
SS. Marcellino e Pietro	Via Merulana, 162
S. Marcello	Piazza S. Marcello
S. Marco	Piazza S. Marco
S. Maria Antigua	Foro Romano
S. Maria d'Ara Coeli	Scala dell'Arce Capitolina, 18

S. Maria degli Angeli	Piazza della Repubblica
S. Maria dell'Anima	Via della Pace, 20
S. Maria della Concezione	Via Veneto
S. Maria della Pace	Via della Pace, 5
S. Maria del Popolo	Piazza del Popolo
S. Maria in Cosmedin	Piazza della Bocca della Verità
S. Maria in Trastevere	Piazza S.Maria in Trastevere
S. Maria in Vallicella	Piazza della Chiesa Nuova
S. Maria in Via Lata	Via del Corso
S. Maria Sopra Minerva	Piazza della Minerva
S. Nicola in Carcere	Via del Teatro Marcello
S. Martino ai Monti	Viale Monte Oppio, 28
S. Onofrio	Piazza S. Onofrio
Pantheon	Piazza della Rotonda
S. Pietro in Montorio	Piazza S. Pietro in Montorio
S. Pietro in Vincoli	Piazza S. Pietro in Vincoli
S. Paolo alle Tre Fontane	Via Laurentina
S. Prassede	Via S. Prassede, 9
S. Prisca	Via S. Prisca 11
S. Pudenziana	Via Urbana 161
SS. Quattro Coronati	Via SS. Quattro Coronati, 20
S. Saba	Piazza G. L. Bernini, 2
S. Sabina	Piazza Pietro di Illiria
S. Silvestro in Capite	Piazza S. Silvestro
S. Sisto Vecchio	Piazzale Numa Pompilio
S. Stefano Rotondo	Via S. Stefano Rotondo
S. Susanna	Via Venti Settembre, 14
Trinita dei Monti	Piazza di Spagna
S. Vitale	Via Nazionale, 194

As for the four patriarchal basilicas: St. Peter's is in the Vatican; Santa Maria Maggiore is in the square by the same name—on the Esquiline hill not far from the railroad station; San Giovanni in Laterano is at the gate called *Porta San Giovanni*; San Paolo Fuori le Mura, St. Paul's Outside The Walls, is out on the Via Ostiense, about two kilometers beyond the Porta San Paolo.

The Major Catacomb Sites

Ciriaca	Piazza S. Lorenzo, 3
Dei Giordani	Via Taro
Domitilla	Via delle Sette Chiese, 282
S. Callisto	Via Appia Antica, 110
S. Agnese	Via Nomentana, 349
Priscilla	Via Salaria 430
S. Sebastiano	Via Appia Antica, 132
S. Felicita	Via Simeto, 2
S. Pancrazio	Piazza S. Pancrazio
Pretestato	Via Appia Pignatelli, 1

APPENDIX II
Latin for Pilgrims

At all papal masses the Creed and the Our Father are sung in Latin. For those pilgrims to Rome who may wish to participate in the singing, here are the two prayers in Latin:

Pater Noster qui es in caelis, sanctificetur nomen tuum: adveniat regnum tuum, fiat voluntas tua, sicut in caelo et in terra. Panem nostrum quotidianum da nobis hodie et dimitte nobis debita nostra, sicut et nos dimittimus debitoribus nostris, et ne nos inducas in tentationem, sed libera nos a malo. Amen

Credo in unum Deum, patrem omnipotentem, factorem caeli et terrae, visibilium omnium et invisibilium. Et in unum Dominum Iesum Christum, Filium Dei unigenitum. Et ex Patre natum ante omnia saecula. Deum de Deo, lumen de lumine, Deum verum de Deo vero. Genitum non factum, consubstantialem Patri: per quem omnia facta sunt. Qui propter nos homines et propter nostram salutem descendit de caelis. Et incarnatus est de Spiritu Sancto ex Maria Virgine: et homo factus est. Crucifixus etiam pro nobis, sub Pontio Pilato passus, et sepultus est. Et resurrexit tertia die, secundum scripturas. Et ascendit in caelum, sedet ad dexteram Patris. Et iterum venturus est cum gloria iudicare vivos et mortuos, cuius regni non erit finis. Et in Spiritum Sanctum, Dominum et vivificantem, qui ex Patre Filioque procedit. Qui cum Patre et Filio simul adoratur et conglorificatur, qui locutus est per Prophetas. Et unum, sanctam, catholicam, et apostolicam Ecclesiam. Confiteor unum baptisma in remissionem peccatorum. Et expecto resurrectionem mortuorum. Et vitam venturi saeculi. Amen

At his Sunday noon appearance, the Holy Father leads the crowds in St. Peter's Square in the recitation of the Angelus. Participation in this requires a knowledge of the Hail Mary and the Gloria Patri in Latin:

> **Ave Maria** gratia plena, Dominus tecum, benedicta tu in mulieribus et benedictus fructus ventris tui, Jesus. Sancta Maria, Mater Dei, ora pro nobis peccatoribus, nunc et in hora mortis nostrae. Amen.

> **Gloria Patri** et Filio et Spiritui Sancto, sicut erat in principio, et nunc et semper, et in saecula saeculorum. Amen.

APPENDIX III
Lenten Station Churches

Pilgrims who find themselves in Rome during the season of Lent may wish to observe the centuries-old practice of *Lenten Stations*. The "Stations," as observed in the earliest times, seems to have consisted of visits by both the clergy and the faithful to the tombs of the martyrs. While the custom dates to the fourth century, it was Pope St. Gregory the Great who, in 590, arranged the rituals to be observed, the churches to be visited and the prayers to be recited.

Gregory intended this devotion to be a means of venerating the relics of our Christian forebears who shed their blood for the faith, and of seeking their intercession for the help the church needs to propagate the gospel. Following is the list of the stations, or churches, established by Pope Gregory:

Ash Wednesday	Santa Sabina
Thursday	San Giorgio in Velabro
Friday	Santi Giovanni e Paolo
Saturday	Sant Agostino
First Sunday in Lent	San Giovanni in Laterano
Monday	San Pietro in Vincoli
Tuesday	Sant Anastasia
Wednesday	Santa Maria Maggiore
Thursday	San Lorenzo in Panisperna
Friday	Santi Apostoli
Saturday	San Pietro
Second Sunday in Lent	Santa Maria in Domnica
Monday	San Clemente
Tuesday	Santa Balbina
Wednesday	Santa Cecilia
Thursday	Santa Maria in Trastevere
Friday	San Vitale

Saturday	Santi Marcellino e Pietro
Third Sunday in Lent	San Lorenzo Fuori Le Mura
Monday	San Marco
Tuesday	Santa Pudenziana
Wednesday	San Sisto
Thursday	Santi Cosmo e Damiano
Friday	San Lorenzo in Lucina
Saturday	Santa Susanna
Fourth Sunday in Lent	Santa Croce in Gerusalemme
Monday	Santi Quattro Coronati
Tuesday	San Lorenzo in Damaso
Wednesday	San Paolo Fuori Le Mura
Thursday	San Martino ai Monti
Friday	Sant Eusebio
Saturday	San Nicola in Carcere
Passion Sunday	San Pietro
Monday	San Crisogono
Tuesday	Santa Maria in Via Lata
Wednesday	San Marcello
Thursday	Sant Apollinare
Friday	San Stefano Rotondo
Saturday	San Giovanni a Porta Latina
Palm Sunday	San Giovanni in Laterano
Monday	Santa Prassede
Tuesday	Santa Prisca
Wednesday	Santa Maria Maggiore
Holy Thursday	San Giovanni in Laterano
Good Friday	Santa Croce in Gerusalemme
Holy Saturday	San Giovanni in Laterano
Easter Sunday	Santa Maria Maggiore

Bibliography

Alimandi, Lia, *Sette Giorni per Sette Colli*. Rome: Alimandi, 1976.

Andrieux, Maurice, *Rome*. New York: Funk and Wagnalls, 1968.

Babou, V., *Civilisation Italienne*. Paris: Didier, 1954.

Bergengruen, Warren, *Rome Remembered*. New York: Herder and Herder, 1968.

Bolton, Glorney, *Roman Century*. New York: Viking, 1970.

Brentano, Robert, *Rome before Avignon*. New York: Basic Books, 1974.

Brown, Blanche, *An Art Guide to Rome*. New York: Doubleday, 1964.

Carcopino, Jerome, *Daily Life in Ancient Rome*. New Haven: Yale University Press, 1940.

Carroll-Abbing, J. Patrick, *But for the Grace of God*. New York: Delacorte Press, 1965.

Chesterton, G. K., *The Resurrection of Rome*. London: Hodder and Stoughton, 1934.

Clark, Eleanor, *Rome and a Villa*. New York: Doubleday, 1952.

Conticello, Baldassare, *Archeology in Rome and Latium*. Novara, Italy: Istituto Geografico, 1985.

Crawford, Marion, *Ave Roma Immortalis*. London: MacMillan & Co., Ltd., 1899.

De Cesare, V., *The Last Days of Papal Rome*. London: Archibald Constable & Co., Ltd., 1909.

Fox, Robin, *Pagans and Christians*. New York: Simon & Schuster, 1989.

Garth, Sheridan, *The Pageant of the Mediterranean*. New York: Hastings House, 1952.

Gessi, Leone, *La Cite du Vatican*. Vatican City: Libreria dello Stato, 1938.

Grant, Michael, *The Jews in the Roman World*. New York: Dorset Press, 1984.

Grisar, Hartmann, *Roma alla Fine del Mondo Antico*. Rome: Desclee & Co., 1943.

Guicciardini, Francesco, *La Storia d'Italia*. Venice: Giorgio Angelieri, 1574.

Hadas, Moses, *A History of Rome*. New York: Doubleday, 1955.

Halperin, William, *Italy and the Vatican at War.* Chicago: University of Chicago Press, 1939.

Hawthorne, Nathaniel, *French and Italian Notebooks.* Boston: Houghton Mifflin & Co., 1871.

Hertling, Ludwig and Englebert Kirschbaum, *The Roman Catacombs and Their Martyrs.* Milwaukee: Bruce Publishing Co., 1956.

Lanciani, Rodolfo, *The Golden Days of the Renaissance in Rome.* New York: Houghton Mifflin & Co., 1906.

―――. *New Tales of Old Rome.* New York: Houghton Mifflin & Co., 1901.

―――. *The Ruins and Excavations of Ancient Rome.* New York: Bell, 1897.

Leon, Harry, *The Jews of Ancient Rome.* Philadelphia: Jewish Publication Society, 1960.

McCormick, Anne O'Hare, *Vatican Journal.* New York: Farrar Strauss, 1957.

Montanelli, Indro, *Storia di Roma.* Milan: Rizzoli, 1957.

Nagle, Brendan, *The Ancient World.* Englewood Cliffs, N.J.: Prentice Hall, 1979.

Northcote, Spencer and W. R. Brownlow, *Roma Sotteranea.* London: Longmans, Green & Co., 1869.

Ravaglioli, Armando, *Il Cuore di Roma.* Rome: Edizioni di Roma, 1984.

Ricci, Corrado, *Roma.* Milano: Fratelli Freves, 1925.

Roberts, Cecil, *And So to Rome.* New York: MacMillan, 1950.

Rothery, Agnes, *Rome Today.* New York: Dodd Mead, 1957.

Showerman, Grant, *Eternal Rome.* New Haven: Yale University Press, 1975.

Story, William, *Roba di Roma.* London: Chapman & Hall, 1871.

Sweeney, Francis, *Vatican Impressions.* New York: Sheed and Ward, 1962.

Tesei, Giovanni, *Le Chiese di Roma.* Rome: Newton Compton, 1991.

Testini, Pasquale, *Le Catacombe e gli Antichi Cimiteri Cristiani in Roma.* Bologna: Cappelli, 1966.

Wiseman, Nicholas, *Fabiola.* New York: P. J. Kenedy, 1914.

Zeppegno, Luciano, *Civilta Sepolte d'Italia.* Milan: Mondadori, 1973.

―――. *I Rioni di Roma.* Rome: Newton Compton, 1978.

Index

Turn page for Mass schedule at Santa Susanna and other books of related interest.

Mass Schedule
at Santa Susanna—
The American Parish
in Rome

(All Masses are in English)

Weekdays: **6:00** P.M.
Saturdays: **6:00** P.M.
Sundays: **9:00 and 10:30** A.M.

MAILING ADDRESS:

The Paulist Fathers
Via Antonio Salandra, 6,
00187 Rome, Italy

PHONE:

Rectory: 06.488.2748 (From the US): 011.3906.488.2748
Fax: 06.474.0236 (From the US): 011.3906.474.0236

Footsteps in Assisi

by Sara Lee Jobe

This collection of poetic reflections and pen-and-ink line drawings of the beautiful Italian town of Assisi introduces readers to the lives, writings and spirituality of Saints Francis and Clare.

"There is a deeply spiritual message in this reflection on the town of Assisi and the lives of St. Francis and St. Clare. Those who read this volume and savor the poetry and the drawings cannot help but hear the gospel message in a new and rich way. It is a Franciscan book, but it is also a very gospel book."

—*Fr. Kenan B. Osborne, O.F.M.*
Franciscan School of Theology
Berkeley, California

ISBN: 0-8091-3635-X   Price $6.95

(Price and availability subject to change)

Ask at your local bookstore.

For more information or to get a
free catalog of our publications, contact us at:

Paulist Press · 997 Macarthur Boulevard · Mahwah, NJ 07430
1-800-218-1903 · Fax: 1-800-836-3161
E-mail: info@paulistpress.com · Visit our website at www.paulistpress.com

WITNESSING THE
HOLY LAND

A PILGRIMAGE IN IMAGE AND WORD
Ellouise Schoettler and James A. Wallace, C.Ss.R.

*The perfect book
for past and future
visitors to the
Holy Land*

Witnessing the Holy Land:
A Pilgrimage in Image and Word

*by Ellouise Schoettler
and James A. Wallace*

The Holy Land is a treasured unity of body and soul, a place where the life of grace is grounded in the reality of the everyday physical world. Inspired by the artist's visit and by the author's sabbatical there, this is a meditation on the Holy Land as presented through word and image.

With poetic text and evocative drawings, *Witnessing the Holy Land* considers such traditional sites as Jerusalem, the Basilica at Nazareth, Bethlehem, the Jordan, Calvary, the Holy Sepulchre and many more. The book is designed with ample white space to become a meditative diary on one's current or past experiences in or expectations of the Holy Land.

This is the perfect book for past and future visitors to the Holy Land, as well as all those who must visit it only in their dreams. It's a must-have for anyone arranging tours, whether through a church office or travel agency or store.

ISBN: 0-8091-3913-8   Price $9.95

(Price and availability subject to change)

Ask at your local bookstore

*For more information or to get a
free catalog of our publications, contact us at:*

**Paulist Press · 997 Macarthur Boulevard · Mahwah, NJ 07430
1-800-218-1903 · Fax: 1-800-836-3161
E-mail: info@paulistpress.com · Visit our website at www.paulistpress.com**

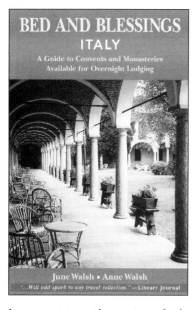